NUNATSUAK

Stories of the Big Land
Labrador and Newfoundland

by
CYRIL GOODYEAR

NUNATSUAK
Stories of the Big Land
Labrador and Newfoundland

by
CYRIL GOODYEAR

CREATIVE PUBLISHERS

St. John's, Newfoundland
2000

THE CANADA COUNCIL | LE CONSEIL DES ARTS
FOR THE ARTS | DU CANADA
SINCE 1957 | DEPUIS 1957

We acknowledge the support of The Canada Council for the Arts for
our publishing program.

We acknowledge the financial support of the Government of Canada
through the Book Publishing Industry Development Program (BPDIP)
for our publishing activities.

Cover photo by Cyril Goodyear

∞ Printed on acid-free paper

Published by

CREATIVE BOOK PUBLISHING

a division of 10366 Newfoundland Limited
a Robinson-Blackmore Printing & Publishing associated company
P.O. Box 8660, St. John's, Newfoundland A1B 3T7

Printed in Canada by:
ROBINSON-BLACKMORE PRINTING & PUBLISHING

Canadian Cataloguing in Publication Data

Goodyear, Cyril, 1926–

Nunatsuak

Selections from the author's column in the
St. John's Evening Telegram, 1986–87.

ISBN 1-894294-16-5

1. Outdoor life — Newfoundland.   2. Goodyear, Cyril, 1926–
I. Title.

GV191.46.N49G66   2000   796.5'092   C00-950024-3

To my wife
Shirley

List of Photographs

Contents

NUNATSUAK

In August 1986 I was appointed to the James G. Channing Fellowship at Memorial University, St. John's, for the academic year 1986-87 which began on September 3rd. At the time I was the Deputy Minister of the Department of Rural, Agricultural and Northern Development of the Government of Newfoundland and Labrador. The Channing Chair, as it is called, was set up by the University and funded by the Government in memory of the late James G. Channing. Mr. Channing was an outstanding public servant, having served successive governments as Clerk of the Executive Council from the time of Confederation with Canada in 1949 until his retirement. Deputy Ministers and public servants with equivalent status were eligible for appointment. It was a sort of sabbatical; appointees taught part time in approved faculties and did research, returning to the public service in a position with equivalent status on completion of their term.

I spent the year in the Political Science Department. With all due respect to members of the Faculty and the University, I have to say that though interesting, the leisurely pace was almost too much for me. For many years I had occupied high stress jobs where life was a constant challenge and hassle, so I looked around for something additional to fill the time. Some people will attest to the fact that without lots of challenging work I can become a trouble maker.

The late Steve Herder of St. John's was Publisher of the *Evening Telegram* at the time, which his family had founded. Since I knew Steve reasonably well, we had a discussion about the possibility of doing a column for the paper. Being no longer with a Government Department, there was no conflict of interest. I was interested in doing an outdoor column with a Labrador connection. The Telegram had an excellent outdoor columnist in the person of Bill Power. Both Steve and I were most anxious that nothing be done to upset him. Bill and I had a talk and I assured him that I would do nothing to undermine his position. It was agreed that I would provide up to three draft columns so that there would never be any conflict with any topic in which he was interested. They always had a surplus from which to choose. The column ran bi-monthly for a year and I enjoyed the exercise.

After a reasonable passage of time, I gave some thought to the idea of putting these columns in a book. On July 11, 1996, Mr. Paul Sparkes, Managing Editor of the *Evening Telegram*, then published by Thomson Canada Limited, granted permission to reprint the columns. I am most grateful to the late Steve Herder for giving me the opportunity to enter the field of amateur journalism. I also wish to thank Mr. Paul Sparkes and Thomson Canada Limited for granting permission to reprint the columns. It speaks well for them that they are willing to give people like me an opportunity to expand our efforts and, hopefully, polish what skills we have.

I wish to express my gratitude to, and appreciation of, my long-suffering spouse, Shirley, who for many years heard these stories ad nauseam and has given me unfailing support in all my undertakings. This book, nor many of the columns, would not have been complete without the outdoor activity in which I participated with Ray Zinck, now retired from the RCMP in Dartmouth, Nova Scotia. Ray has been my long time hunting, fishing and canoeing buddy; a fellow "Labra-dorian." I also owe a great debt to many of the people mentioned in this book. On the face of it, some of the stories may not seem too complimentary to those mentioned; I mean no harm. They are part of the mix of people who make our society what it is, and who make it tick. They are also not the people historians write about; that is what makes history so artificial. We have been conditioned to believe that the stuff in history is the activities and antics of royalty and politicians. However, that gives a false picture. It is people like those in this book who make things work and make society what it is; an ever-changing drama of real life. I have learned much from these people and I appreciate and understand why they acted as they did.

My thanks also go to Creative Book Publishing. I thank, in particular, Don Morgan, Heather Tucker and Dwayne LaFitte who had the nerve to take a chance on this book.

I donate all royalties from this book to The Eric Normore Memorial Foundation in Deer Lake. The foundation was established to perpetuate the memory of one of our many war heroes. Its overall purpose is to improve the quality of life in Deer Lake and nearby areas.

Some of the columns have been dropped. All have been rewritten and polished to some extent, since columns have to be tailored with an economy of words to fit into the space available in a newspaper. Some new material has been added to fill the space between the covers. With some fictional exceptions, all of the characters are real and each one taught me a lesson which I hope old age won't cause me to forget. I pass them onto you in the hope that you will enjoy this mixed bag of memories. If you are amazed at the feats of some of the characters, amused at the antics of others, saddened by the fate of some, enlightened by the ingenuity and culture of many; this will have been worthwhile. Pick up this little book and put it down at will.

—*Cyril J. Goodyear,*
Deer Lake, Nfld.
January 19th, 2000.

THE MEANING OF NUNATSUAK

Nunatsuak; what a strange name! How do you pronounce it? Why, phonetically of course. Nu-nat-su-ak, Nu-nat-su-ak; just speed it up a little and you have NUNATSUAK. What Progress! Go to the head of the class.

Ok, now you know how to pronounce it but still don't know what it is. Is it an exotic food? A drink perhaps, or a figment of the imagination of some advertising executive? Wrong on all counts. It's an Inuit word (perhaps Eskimo to you) and roughly translated means "the big land." It's interesting to note that Alaska has the same general meaning. The Inuit language (inuktitut) is capable of embracing the most minute and particular description, as well as extremely difficult concepts. Sometimes these can be expressed by one word, like Nunatsuak. Words are sometimes more meaningful to the speaker than the listener. For example, the experienced Inuit outdoors man knows that Nunatsuak and "environment" as we explain it, are only remotely related.

When an Inuit utters the word Nunatsuak, one has a conceptual and mental image which is more than his immediate universe. It is more than lakes and rivers, mountains and barrens, caribou and seal, char and cod. He sees sea ice as land and would only consider places like Davis Inlet as an island during the summer when it is actually surrounded by water. So to the Inuit, Davis Inlet is only nine miles from Sangu Bay by land for seven or eight months of the year. Not only does he see the totality of these things in his mind, but feels what the word Nunatsuak can only express to him: a special relationship with the land and water and the creatures that reside within it. The wind, frost, rain and snow have their special place in the blend of things. While weather may bring some discomfort, it is never the expensive nuisance that it is to the city dweller.

I have a tremendous respect for the Inuit, though not all individuals fall within the ambit of that respect. Their culture has produced the best in outdoor technique and design. Indians (Innu) share in the special feeling for the earth and have produced cultures as varied as the areas in which they live. However, it takes a special type of person to survive in "Nunatsuak."

That special feeling for "the big land" is not exclusively ethnic. There are some of us to whom Nunatsuak is a concept, reality and a feeling difficult to put into words. It is for those who share Nunatsuak, to whatever degree, that this collection of stories is written. Sometimes the relationship to what is perceived as "the outdoors" will be rather tenuous; some of the stories will be anecdotal. If the subject is an animal, it won't look like it has been lifted from an encyclopedia. There will be stories about stalking seals with a Telluk, salmon fishing on the Hunt River, tenting at thirty below zero, climbing Mount Sylvester, arresting Santa Claus, Zane Grey's cabin on the Codroy, canoeing the Bay du Nord, characters I have met, and a host of others.

I hope that there will be something of interest for everyone who shares that love of "the big land." Age, gender and physical condition shouldn't have anything to do with it. Last of all, I hope to highlight a few lessons that I learned and try to bring about a better understanding between the people of Newfoundland and Labrador. If others get to know us better, it will be a bonus.

LABRADOR STORIES

THE HUNT RIVER

I had a friend some years ago who used to get bored catching salmon. Hard to believe, isn't it? On one occasion he was fishing a certain river in Labrador when boredom pressed heavily upon him. While casting about for something to do, he spotted several gulls hovering around the salmon pools. He caught a salmon parr and, snipping off the fly, tied the fish to his leader. Next, he stripped off about a hundred yards of line, coiling it loosely on the beach, and then lay down with the rod, behind a big rock. Soon a gull noticed the fish; swooped in — and away. My friend played that seagull in the sky until the bewildered bird let the fish go. Now, who's gullible?

Between Hopedale and Davis Inlet is Big Bay, and into it flows the Hunt River. It has many salmon pools, all the way from the tidal area to the Falls and beyond. The Anglo-Newfoundland Development Company used to own the fish camp there on the island, not far from the tidal water. From it, you can look up toward Trout Pool, formed where the brook flows out from Grassy Lake and joins the main river; a fisherman's dream. That camp has since passed into other hands, but the river continues to fulfil the ambitions and memories of many people. I am one of them.

One summer the camp was idle and Bert Patey and I went in for the late fishing and early waterfowl hunting. Bert, a good outdoors man, used to live in Goose Bay. Nowadays he and Maggie live officially in Sandy Cove, Newfoundland, near Eastport, but really only come back there occasionally in order to decide where to go next.

Roland Vivian of Glenwood, now deceased, was chief guide for the Company. At that time he was really acting as caretaker for the camp, as there were no guests. He was a fine, modest man, competent in every way, and I am proud to have had him for a friend.

When we arrived we told Rollie he was now the guest. I did the cooking and Bert the chores. We brought in everything except a boat, as there was one for every pool. It was a pleasure to remind Rollie that he had nothing to do for a change, except play the 'sport.' There were noble feeds, elastic yarns, and if you had been there you could have heard the laughter drown out the roar of the river.

The first morning I slipped out early to the nearest pool. I just managed to strip off a little line before I heard Patey thump by in his brand-new chest waders. Within minutes he was on his way back to the cabin, making a different sound. When queried, he admitted slipping down the muddy bank into the river; a total immersion course in salmon fishing.

Trout Pool is just that; filled with big trout, interspersed with salmon. At the lower end it is quite deep, and a rocky reef provides a drop-off from which to fish. Above the pool there is a shallow semi-rapid, full of deep roundish holes. The salmon lie in them, up towards a small island. Above this is another pool. If you are wading and get distracted, it is easy to drop in over your head.

I was fishing a hole just off the island, and watching Bert trying not to catch the big trout which constantly came for the fly. That is what you have to do, if you want to catch salmon. Each time he hauled away, the backcast dropped the fly over a deep hole not far from me. Imagine his surprise when he tried to cast out and he couldn't; he'd hooked a small salmon on the backcast and had to turn around to play it. It's the first and only time I have ever seen that happen. Maybe Guinness will show that Patey holds the record.

On the weekend a group, who shall remain nameless, arrived in from Goose Bay. We now became the guides for them. After they landed, the good fishing weather set in; not fit for a dog! However, the fish didn't mind; they're always wet. I made a huge pot of salmon and trout chowder; so thick it had to be stirred with a stout alder. A certain person lost his trophy trout in that chowder. We also barbecued steaks, brought in from Goose of course. By dropping them on the ground occasionally, the flavour was improved: a good time was had by all.

We fished for two weeks; sometimes from the boats, other times wading. Rarely did we fish the same pool after catching a salmon; just moved onto the next pool. There was no one else on the river. It was a pleasure just to be the guide for the other two.

Sitting in the stern of the boat, dropping it slowly down the pool on the anchor line while Rollie cast expertly, reminded me of how careful you have to be when someone is behind you. Rollie told me of a time on the same river when he came up to check on the other guides and their sports. As he waded around a point, he saw a fisherman in the bow happily slashing his line back and forth. In the stern sat the guide, hunched over, with a plastic beef bucket hauled over his head.

You have no doubt heard all kinds of stories about salmon fishing; how the water temperature should be within a certain range; how the weather and lighting conditions should be ideal. Well, all those excuses for not catching salmon disappear in Labrador. We caught salmon in all weather, the worse the better; at all times of the day, and when it was cold enough to skin you, with ice making around shore. There is a high degree of satisfaction in hooking a salmon in a tidal pool when everyone else has given up for the season. These salmon are still covered with sea lice; proving how late they run.

When you come ashore to the campfire under the bank, warm your numbed hands and rear, see the swift ducks shear off when they spot your buddy in the pool, visualize the good meal you'll have in an hour or two; man, you've arrived!

Hunting the Hunt

Having arranged for our hunting licenses before leaving Goose Bay, we decided to go up the brook to Grassy Lake. Grassy Lake brook flows into the Trout Pool on the Hunt River. The season was now open for ducks and geese and we had seen and heard them continuously. One of the reasons I like the canoe even more, is the experience of struggling a Gander Bay boat* up to Grassy Lake. The September weather was beautiful and the ducks, not having seen human beings like us, were easy prey; but then, Patey was always a quack shot. The upper part of the brook is a series of steadies, ideal for ducks. We almost silently eased around the bends, and bagged them.

Into a bowl in the hills we pushed the boat and, rounding a bend in the brook, came upon Grassy Lake. It is well named, shallow of water, with coarse grass growing everywhere, and mud right down to China. It is a haven for trout, and

---

* An oversized local version of a canoe, some 18 to 22 feet in length, with a V-shaped stern capable of carrying a 25hp outboard motor.

The Falls — Hunt River, 1989

Heap Big Smoke — Trout Pool bank — Hunt River, 1989

undoubtedly the homestead of those in the Trout Pool. A beautiful place — the peace broken only by us.

With a good bag of ducks and evening coming on, we looked for a place to camp. We had taken only a small tarp and some food, so a sheltered campsite was necessary. On the north side of the lake we found a big old spreading spruce, with limbs right to the ground; nature's umbrella. There was a well-beaten path around the lake and leading up to the tree. From the droppings it was plain that a bear was using the tree for shelter, following forays around the lake.

We cut bough brooms and left 'bearly' a trace of the former occupant. With a fire going and supper on, I took a walk around the bear path. In the half light, the mirror water and the column of smoke above the trees and cliff face was a soul-satisfying sight; never to be forgotten. The bear didn't come back that night, and we'll never know why. Perhaps it was a combination of the earlier gunshots, the fire and Patey's snoring.

I won't bore you with the details of the fish and fowl we got at Grassy Lake. Let us rather talk of the river which flows out of Char Lake into Big Bay. It is farther out the Bay from the mouth of the Hunt River. What a terrific arctic char river, and the flats at the mouth are both a breeding ground and a staging area for geese. In August we had built three driftwood blinds there, suitably spaced. It would have been better if we had built them in the spring so that the geese would now be accustomed to them.

Geese are super intelligent, and wary. They always scan an area before landing, and post guards after. They are highly organized and very successful in evading hunters. I have watched them for hours, and the most success was in learning how they act. Aside from building blinds too late in the season, many hunters camp near the hunting area. The eagle-scout geese spot them, and shear off somewhere else. We sought to avoid that by not taking any camping gear. Our intention was to hide the boat after we came down the bay to the river. We would carry only enough to eat, and keep partly warm. You always hope the end result will justify the discomfort. After all, who ever got a goose when sitting in a comfortable living room?

It was now cold at night and ice made around the shore; a time to look to your back and belly. One of Patey's passing planes dropped off a few things, including a huge roast. Rollie cooked it in the propane oven in the main cabin and I made it into three oversized sandwiches. Thus provisioned we headed out the bay. The tide was in, so we hid the boat and waited for the right time to get into the blinds. The geese could be heard in conversation on the far side of the big island. You can't boil up on such occasions, so we swallowed a dry lunch, saving the sandwiches for later. About midnight each of us went into his blind.

Early in the morning I was lying in my blind, tight to the water, wearing two parkas, long underwear and heavy pants, waders, wool cap and mitts and rolled up in a tarp; it was cold out there! My mind revolved around everything it could, but still the dawn was far away. When the moon finally came up over the water the geese could be heard, but not seen. Contemplating that sandwich, I heard a flutter; there on the driftwood above my head was an owl, wide-eyed with astonishment. I was about to ask, "whoo are you?" when loud snores came over the water. That bird wisely flew away. I shivered out of the tarp and ate the super roast beef sandwich. Dawn finally came, but no geese. There are several probable explanations, not the least of which were those unearthly snores. Anyway, I have so much respect for geese that I don't mind being outwitted by them

September is a beautiful time of the year, wherever you are. Steaming back up the bay to the river without geese, the cold spray in your face, hungry but heading for that warm cabin, convinces you that it is good to be alive. How else would you have the sensitivity to feel so miserable? You see, even discomfort comes from being alive. We all need to feel it from time to time to appreciate that fact.

During the last two days we fished the lower pools. Salmon were still running in with the rising tides. The two we ate those last evenings were bright and firm; gourmet food when boiled with a chunk of salt beef.

I stood outside that last night, called by nature, and listened to the symphony of intermingled sounds of wind, trees, river and the occasional conversation of geese. Clouds scudded across the moon, momentarily brightening the lantern-lit window of the cabin. An involuntary shiver reminded me it was time to crawl into that down bag, and contemplate the next trip to the Hunt.

A BUNDLE OF SPLITS

Imagine you are camped in the wilderness in Labrador in early March. Except for the sunny days, winter is all around you. Go into the tent, have a seat on the bed and lean your back against the standing tree at the rear. That tree, and its partner at the front, keep up the ridge pole. There's no room for chairs, even if you needed them. Throw your parka, cap and mitts in the hammock-like net which runs the length of the peak inside. They will be warm and dry when you go out, and won't take up floor space in the meantime. The floor is snowshoe-tamped and layered with spruce boughs; stain master carpet! Unlike summer tents, this one does not have a canvas floor. The bed is part of the floor, covered with a light tarp, a foam pad and eiderdown sleeping bag. It runs along the back wall and from it you can access the stove, and look out the door. The bag has a winter shuck with a large pocket on top for odds and ends. It also has a hood to stop the draft if you're really 'bare' headed. A jogging fleece liner adds to the comfort. If you fear rolling out of bed, just place a log along the outer edge, and keep it in place by driving a peg into the snow at each end.

The sheet iron stove, measuring 8 x 8 x 24 inches, is cherry red and strong light flickers from the draft hole in the door. By placing the stove at right angles to the bed, with the pipe slanted out the front wall beside the door opening, a canvas fly can be placed over the roof. It also facilitates kicking the stove out the front door if an accident occurs. You can smell the heated wood piled under and around the stove. The wood under the stove prevents the 'floor' from melting. Dry splits and birch rhind are right by the head of the bed, so you can reach out and light the fire in the morning without getting up. The kettle sings and the stew bubbles, giving out odours more powerful than heated wood, or the odd back draft of smoke through the open tent door. Don't knock over the candle at your elbow! The candle stick is driven in the floor. A strip of birch rhind in the partly split stick holds the candle at a convenient level; but you have to watch it. However, it is completely adjustable if you want to move it over, up or down. Here, mix yourself a hot toddy, if you like, or a cup of tea; supper will be ready soon.

How come there's no draft? Well, the light nylon snow-cloth sewn around the bottom of the tent walls is boughed down on the packed snow. Sure, the tent door is open, but the stove provides a heat-lock. Also, there is never any condensation in a well-ventilated tent; all body and cooking moisture flows straight outside. A good canvas fly over the roof keeps the heat inside. The woods around you also provide shelter. All things are relative; perhaps you can remember the many times you walked down a windy or rain-swept street? What a difference it made when you ducked into a doorway.

What comfort, how pleasant; not at all like you imagined. How nice to sit and look out at the moonlight sparkling on the snow, watch the shadows dance alongside the moving trees, and hear the wind coming toward you through the boughs.

You will sleep like a baby, even when the fire goes out; eat like a horse, after snowshoeing and cutting wood; and lie around like a dog when the day is over. You will hate to leave it, eh?

But comfort is not a natural phenomenon; it has to be planned and created. The difference between comfort and discomfort, in any climate, is clothing and housing. However, intelligent application is the key; it doesn't always require much physical effort, unless problems are created.

I remember one December, years ago, just before Christmas, a now prominent friend and I went partridge hunting up along the Churchill River. It was thirty-eight below zero,

Fahrenheit, when we left. There was no wind, but snowmobiles create their own wind and we had to stop frequently to check for frozen faces. We camped near the mouth of Lower Brook on the Churchill River, about twenty-five miles from Goose Bay. The tent was set up between two standing trees; that way you have to cut only one pole. Enough wood was cut and split for a couple of days. Dry wood was really scarce, as that area has always been popular for camping. We had enough splits to start the fire twice, with a couple of small junks left over. The next day I planned to look for a few more sticks of dry wood. The Indians used to cut trees and stand them against others to dry, in case they needed them sometime. Unfortunately, not too many do that any more; they only burn whatever they find.

We hunted for a while and got a couple of ptarmigan; darkness came early. After a big feed, we turned in as we say. In extremely cold weather I always put on a fresh pair of homespun (or down) socks and a suit of padded underwear. It makes it easier to turn over in the sleeping bag, and increases the warmth of the bag. Every other article of clothing goes up in the loft-net, where it catches the first morning heat from the stove.

My friend didn't change his socks and apparently didn't sleep very comfortably. Several times, when I was awakened by the sharp reports of trees splitting in the frost, I heard him rooting at the stove. That didn't bother me because there was lots of green wood, if the fire was kept going. I put him nearest the stove for that reason.

When I awoke in the morning, it was bitterly cold and the fire was out. A ten-ounce cotton duck canvas tent does not keep out much cold in those temperatures. To my consternation, every split was gone; there was nothing left to light the fire. Well, sir or ma'am, as the case may be; if it wasn't for the problem of explaining to his widow and others; I could have made away with him right then.

He was now sound asleep. I got up, put on my icy clothing, and snowshoed up a gully for about a quarter of a mile before I found two dry trees. By the time I got them back to the tent, cut and split the wood, my hands were almost useless. My friend got up and dressed in the warm tent, while I cooked breakfast.

I gave him a bundle of splits for Christmas. We often laugh about it now.

UNCLE JOHNNIE WALKS TO GOOSE

It's March 9ᵗʰ,1987 and I'm camped between the Gander Bay Road and the Gander River. I've just begun a week of rabbit catching and ice fishing. Snowshoes provide transportation from the tent to the slips and the pond. It is warm and comfortable in my tent and, looking out through the open door, the moon is as bright as day. Contributing to that good feeling is a deer steak and trimmings, which I just managed to get down. What could be better than eating a deer steak from Nova Scotia in woods full of moose. It is nice to be alone and away from the all the stresses of work.

The tent stove is cherry red and I have to pour away some precious water because the spruce stove legs have started to smoke. There is no water where I'm camped and snow has to be melted for cooking. Ever hear of waterless cooking? Well, this is waterless living. One time it was a luxury to be clean, now it's a luxury to be dirty. You have to be able to afford poverty.

Every time I look at that stove I think of Uncle Johnnie Broomfield. He made it for me in 1968. With reasonable care it will last a long time. It is a work of art and I hope it churns out meals for another twenty years. A good tent stove is hard to come by; they are either too big, too heavy or don't draw anything but constant attention. Uncle Johnnie was a master tinsmith. His designs, especially for camping gear, embodied many years of experience in winter camping. For months on end his tent was his home, especially when he and others founded Happy Valley, the civilian settlement next to Goose Air Base in Labrador.

His forebears came to Labrador with the Hudson's Bay Company, like many of the early settlers, and his home was in

Big Bay, near Davis Inlet. There he spent his early years fishing, hunting and trapping. In those days a family occupied a bay and it comprised almost the known world to them. The great depression was during most of his early life, times were hard and wage employment almost non existent. What a blessing it would be to break the credit cycle. People could hardly believe it when they heard an air base was being built in Goose Bay and jobs were available. There are still many left who know what a godsend the military base has been. I wonder what Uncle Johnnie would say now if he was aware of the big fuss about low level flying?

The base started in the summer of 1941 in the dark days of the War and was intended as both a defensive establishment, and a short cut for ferrying aircraft to England. In 1939, 1940 and the winter of 1941-42, the fishery and trapping industry were a disaster on the north coast of Labrador. Many people were desperate and, with all political and economic effort focused on the War, forgotten. Around the middle of April, Uncle Johnnie left Big Bay to meet with others and travel to Goose Bay. Between Big Bay and Makkovik the job seekers swelled to fifteen.

They all had dog-teams, but they walked. Forget about all that romantic stuff you've been led to believe about dog-team travel. The dogs haul your gear, but mainly you walk. At best you jog, if for no other reason than to keep warm. On long trips the pace is slow, slower if the snow is deep, or rotten as it is in the spring. In the early morning there is a crust on the snow but as the day wears on dogs and people break through. The crust is sharp and I've seen dog legs skinned and bleeding from repeatedly breaking through. Some people put skin boots on their dogs, but while it prevented injury it did nothing for the pace.

Also, crossing the bays and lakes there is slob and water. On the bays, when the tide falls, all that water collects in the middle where the ice has 'belled' down. Seaweed and debris in, or on, the ice causes more rapid melting in spring and

A typical dog team, Nain, 1946-47

leaves treacherous holes. It all added up to numbed feet and legs as Uncle Johnnie and his companions repeatedly went over their sealskin boots. The icy water added to the crippling of the dog's feet and legs. Why did they do it? They needed work and knew work would not come to them. There were no bush planes then. The only way to get there was to walk, jog, ride occasionally; or travel by boat in summer. Otherwise it was stay home and go hungry.

Their route to Goose Bay was:-
Big Bay to Davis Inlet — day one.
Davis Inlet to Hopedale — day two.
Hopedale to Makkovik — day three.
Makkovik to Tuchialik — day four.
Tuchialik to Ticoraluk — day five.
Ticoraluk to Rigolet — day six
Rigolet to Vallies Bight — day seven
Vallies Bight to Mulligan — day eight
Mulligan to Northwest River — day nine
Northwest River to Otter Creek — day ten

They arrived on April 25th, 1942. Look at the map of Labrador and see how far they travelled. Please bear in mind that dog-team travel is not straight-line miles — or kilometres, as we like to say in Canada.

Seven gruelling, brutal days down the coast from Davis Inlet to Rigolet and ninety miles up Lake Melville to Otter Creek, Goose Bay. Across the bays, over the necks of land, across the rivers and through the woods; endless expanses of ice and snow. Imagine a bay, ten miles wide and there you are moving virtually at a snails pace with the distant point never seeming to get nearer. Walk, snowshoe, untangle the dogs, haul them back every time they split around a rock or tree, span the cracks in the ice and hope to God you don't fall in. All this broken by boiling the kettle now and then, setting up the tent when necessary, and hoping some kind stranger will take you in for the night; which they always did. Uncle Johnnie and his companions always found something to laugh about; humour keeps everyone going.

All this pain, wearying effort for a job they didn't have, hoping to find work they probably couldn't perform. They were jacks-of-all trades but had no provable skills. Their would-be employers were foreigners, and they were refugees in their own country; people have become famous for lesser feats.

At Otter Creek Uncle Johnnie saw his first truck. It could only travel around the newly constructed area. When he told these strangers where they had come from and why, they were immediately hired as labourers. What a catastrophe if it had been otherwise, for at Northwest River they had sold their dogs and gear in order to get enough money to continue.

Uncle Johnnie told me this story many times, not always in full, or even in sequence. In his modest way he would use episodes to illustrate what he was trying to put across.

As with many careers, where circumstances dictate events, Uncle Johnnie became a tinsmith because he got to the stage where he wanted to work inside. He had endured his share of the cold. When the Americans offered him a job as helper in the base tinsmith shop he was 'galvanized' into action. The job appealed to him as he saw how tent stoves and other outdoor gear could be made, if you knew how and had the equipment. He'd had his fill of cobbled up work.

While his academic achievements were limited, Uncle Johnnie was undaunted. He took a correspondence course in sheet metal work in order to cope with mathematics and design. His efforts were rewarded because he became foreman of the sheet metal shop on Goose Air Base. You might say 'he walked into the job.'

In his spare time, Uncle Johnnie worked hard at being one of the founding fathers of Happy Valley. He was also one of the founders of the Moravian Church there, and an Elder. With his job and all the rest going on, he built his own house. In between he learned to play several musical instruments. I remember travelling with him on the coastal boat from Goose to Davis Inlet. Every evening, by popular request, he rocked the music room with his renditions on the piano. It just goes to show what you can do, when you try. I have to say that Uncle Johnnie Broomfield was a gentleman of the first order.

Uncle Johnnie passed away on February 22, 1976, at the age of sixty-seven. He walked to Goose and spent much of his life there, but his heart was always in Big Bay, Labrador. Though small in stature, he was a giant in many ways.

It is not only your stove that provides me with comfort, Uncle Johnnie. I remember you most vividly for your drive and energy, your modesty, kindness and wisdom; and your epic journey. My memories are most vivid when I am camped at Lower Brook, Mulligan, Flower's Bay, Goose Arm, Gander Bay and a hundred other places.

IT TAKES PULL

Uncle Isaac Rich was not well known outside Labrador; what a pity! He was an old-time trapper, like his contemporaries and ancestors, but he ended up working for the Yanks on Goose Air Base. When I first met him he was retired; from the Base, that is. He went back into the woods and did all kinds of other things that made us, and him, forget he was getting old. There was a lot of tragedy in his life; only the strong can survive without bitterness.

My buddy Ray Zinck and I spent many a pleasant hour talking to him at his home in Happy Valley. Mrs. Rich would sit nearby sewing or knitting, and would nod agreement now and then. She had a man to be proud of, and it was obvious that the feeling was mutual.

Uncle Ike was a philosopher in the true sense. His life experiences and his keen mind had made him so. Unlike many of his contemporaries, he could articulate those thoughts and experiences. He had never heard of Aristotle, Socrates or Plato and, unlike them, didn't have the luxury of relaxing in sunny Mediterranean surroundings. The impressions he left are no less indelible than theirs.

Before the Americans came to Goose Bay, the mainstay of people in that region was trapping and fishing. People from Mud Lake, Northwest River, Mulligan and Rigolet trapped and fished the great waterways that flow into Lake Melville. Some of them trapped the upper reaches and tributaries of the Grand River, which has been renamed the Churchill. They went by canoe in the fall of the year to the Unknown River, in the vicinity of Twin Falls and near Churchill Falls. That is about two hundred miles, against the current all the way, and before outboard motors became available. Uncle Ike was one of them. Most of them would come down for Christmas, towing a toboggan full of furs. Canoes were left up there for the return trip in the spring. After Christmas they would go back up to their trapping grounds, travelling on snowshoes and hauling a toboggan loaded with supplies and gear. There were no luxuries on those toboggans. That is a long pull with about 150 pounds, at temperatures sometimes down to forty below zero and beyond. At those temperatures trees will split, and you'd swear it was a rifle shot. So, up in the fall, down at Christmas, up after Christmas, and back in the spring; that is about eight hundred miles.

We talked about those feats many times; feats of endurance to us, but normal and necessary to them. Now, you can talk and read about something, but never know what it is really like until you do it yourself. It may be a bit crazy, but then how many irrational things have we done?

Zinck and I got two eight-foot toboggans and made harnesses similar to those you make for a dog. The lead lines were also about eight feet. By splitting the gear; tent, stove, sleeping bags, spare clothing, boots, food and implements, we had about a hundred and ten pounds each. It pays to do a trial run, and this was done back of the Spruce Park housing area in Goose Bay. It was not very dignified for the Judge; but people get used to your antics after a while.

Around the middle of February we made a long weekend of it. We drove to a point on the Northwest River road and lashed the gear on the toboggans. Now I know what 'working like a dog' means. The central region of Labrador is heavy snow country, and that old snow was piled up on the limbs of the spruce trees. I don't know how many times the toboggans disappeared when turning close in between the trees. Less restrained people would have been forced to utter a word of prayer.

It is amazing how little clothing you need to wear when

snowshoeing and pulling a loaded toboggan. Regardless, you'd better have your hood up and ready to ward off bough loads of snow.

Between the Northwest River road and Grand Lake, there is some really rough terrain, but beautiful in winter. There is a chain of small lakes which run roughly parallel to the road and well in towards Grand Lake. One of these was our destination, and we would follow these lakes and circle back out; sixteen miles by the map.

We set up camp late that afternoon on a point overlooking the biggest lake. You may not believe it but we barely had enough strength left to chop enough wood for the weekend. However, it's surprising what lots of tea and a couple of lunches will do to revive you while waiting for supper to cook.

Sunday was a day of rest, as prescribed; a time to ease your back and contemplate whether you're crazy or not. After a sumptuous breakfast of seal meat, gravy, toast and coffee the world began to look better. Sitting back in the tent with a nice fire on, while the starving jays came right in after the scraps, makes you realize that comfort and contentment have no particular setting.

By the time we got back to Goose Bay we had some appreciation of what trappers endured, and the satisfaction of having done it. This country was built by people like Uncle Ike Rich, not professional philosophers and engineers. Each has his contribution to make in his own time, but articulated thoughts are not always based on reality and experience. I don't know if you are in the same place as Aristotle, Socrates and Plato, Uncle Ike; but if you are, they can learn a lot from you.

INGENUITY — LOCAL STYLE

The following is like the story about a fellow who is reported to have said, "Yesterday I couldn't spell ex-ec-u-tive, and now I are one."

Then there's the other one about an outport merchant who was very proud of the fact that his son was the first one from the community to go to college. That was before Memorial became a university. The son was home for the holidays and his father took him to the weekly meeting at the Orange Lodge. Before the meeting started he took his son around to speak to the other members, boasting about all he had learned. To make his point he said, "Son, say something in algebra or geometry." "Trying to avoid embarrassing his father the boy said, "pi-r^2." One old fellow looked up and said, "Me son, you better go back to school because everybody knows cake are squared and pie are round."

Ingenuity was only understood by the so-called educated years ago. Most people would not have been able to spell it, let alone define it. However, since Confederation, and with the advent of Scrabble, most people now know it means 'using your brains.' Many people knew how to do that before Confederation. A lot of us have been hampered since by too strict adherence to the standards of formal education.

I remember one time making a box for my gas lantern, and spent about an hour trying to accommodate the handle. My spouse came along and said, "Why don't you fold it down the side and put the thing in corner-wise?" I'm still trying to figure out whether 'stunness' is endemic or academic.

The Sawmill

Let us see if you can saw! There is a chap in Port Hope Simpson, Labrador who, amongst other things, is a good boat builder. However, he found it difficult to get planks for his boats as he couldn't afford a proper mill. He got a mill saw, made a carriage and bought a wrecked car. By putting a drive belt on a rear wheel he could run the saw. Unfortunately, the thing moved when operating and the belt slipped. He compensated for this by attaching a stout rope to each end of the bumper, tied them to a tree, twisted them with a stick, and kept proper tension on the belt. The car trunk and body stored tools and other necessary items. By paying $50.00 for a car wreck, he kept on building boats and selling them at a reasonable price. One could observe that the wrecks caused the boats to float.

Going to Pot

Seigfried Hettesch was the Moravian Missionary in Makkovik. Once on a caribou hunting trip he blew the cylinder head gasket on his snowmobile. At that time they were made of aluminum. He was born in Labrador and learned how to use his brains. He cut the bottom out of an aluminum pot, replaced the gasket, and drove back home. That could be called 'engine-uity.' Seig was the kind of guy who could do almost anything. He once even made false teeth. I have to smile when I think of them because he never did quite bridge the gap between denturist and dentist.

The Net

The idea of setting a net under the ice is enough to strain any brain. The genius of the Northerner is certainly well demonstrated in that exercise. Although the technique, now seldom used, is not confined to Labrador, however it is the only place I have ever seen it.

First you lay out the net on the ice. Next you cut two long poles. Depending on the length of the net and the poles, you determine how many holes have to be cut in the ice. The holes are best cut with an axe as they need to be oblong. When you finish the mildly exerting exercise of cutting the holes you tie the two poles at one end; like shear-poles for a winter tent. Next, tie a long rope to the other end of one pole and push the other pole down the first hole. By working the first pole, you line up the second pole with the next hole. Push down the first pole and the second will float up through the hole, sufficient to pull it up. It helps to have a buddy.

Pull the poles through the hole and repeat the cold, painstaking, process until you haul the poles up through the last hole. All you have to do now is untie the poles, tie on the net and pull it through to its end. The net is now suspended in the water under the ice. Each end of the rope is tied to a tree or rock on shore, or a stick frozen in the ice. Securing the latter is simple; just chop down far enough so that some water comes up, tie your line to a stick and push it in the hole. The stick will freeze in as solidly as an anchor; nothing to it!

The rope must be long enough so that you can provide enough slack to pull the net back up through the hole at one end. Usually char and large trout are caught. These are fresh frozen not long after they are taken from the net and dropped on the ice. Whatever ice makes on the net as you haul it will fall off when you pull it back under water. That is a well-known phenomenon to old-timer loggers and trappers who years ago used to put their vegetables in a burlap bag, tie a rope to a tree, and drop the bag into the pond or brook. Vegetables never freeze while in the water.

Therapy

Some years ago I attended a meeting in Hopedale to discuss relocation of the village to another site. It was much like the current situation in Davis Inlet. Many reasons were given for moving, most of them invalid. One person said his reason was that there was no supply of firewood nearby. In the heat of the discussion Chesley Flowers remarked, "Those that got no

wood now, wouldn't have no wood if they lived in the woods."
He, of course, was opposed to moving.

It takes a lot of energy and initiative to live in Hopedale,
perhaps not as much as years ago, but it still does not have as
many advantages as most places. One of the most able people
there was Chesley Flowers. He moved there years ago from
Flowers Bay; named after his forebears. Even after he retired,
so to speak, he was still one of the best hunters, trappers,
carvers and handymen I have ever seen. My spouse said he
had the bluest eyes she ever saw. Behind them was a fine
intellect.

Late one fall his son failed to return from a hunting trip.
The weather was terrible and no one was willing to begin a
search until the storm abated. Chesley went out alone and
finally spotted a fire on a small island some distance from
Hopedale. There was no safe way he could get the big boat in
to pick up the boy as it was on a windward shore. He dropped
an anchor off the stern and paid out the rope so that the boat
would not go aground. In the process, on that terrible night,
his leg became entangled in the rope and his knee was almost
pulled out of its socket. Despite this, he got his son aboard
and they made it back to Hopedale.

Chesley spent a long time recovering. While doing so he
carved several hundred dollars worth of soapstone. We have
two pieces; one is an Inuit woman scraping a sealskin, the
other is a polar bear eating a seal. The polar bear even has a
set of ivory teeth, which Chesley carved. Perhaps he learned
that last technique from Seigfried Hettesch. After, when he
was able to hobble around, he built and sold sixteen koma-
tiks.* If you could have got him to talk, he would have said
these activities were the best possible therapy.

It is necessary to take poetic license here, and apologize
to whoever wrote the other version.

> "Full many a flower is born to bloom unseen,
>   and use his talents in the clear cold air."

---

* Innuite two-runner sleigh, from twelve to twenty feet in length.

STALKING AN UTUK

Hunting has been away of life in Newfoundland and Labrador for centuries. That is so with many societies where the difficulties of transportation delayed the arrival of the supermarket. Interest in and dependency on hunting rises in direct proportion to isolation and the lack of readily available fresh foods. Of course hunting and outdoor living generally have tremendous appeal, even to the affluent. Every effort should be made to encourage development of those basic skills. People without them will not fare well in the event of a major natural or man-made disaster.

Stalking game, even with good cover and top grade weapons, requires great skill and ability. How much more so when there is no cover and few weapons! Old Boas Obed said that "necessity is the mother of invention." Maybe it wasn't him, but the Inuit, like the rest of us, had more than their share of necessity in the old days. Out of that necessity came many inventions. One of them was the Telluk.

Of course you know the Telluk. I can see the picture in your mind's eye of a fur clad figure out there in the middle of a white nowhere. He stands on a scrap of polar bear skin, harpoon poised, waiting for the raven's feather to move in the crust over the seal's blow hole. That is the wrong picture because by now the Inuit had acquired the rifle from the Hudson's Bay Company.

It is spring; late March, April or May. Out there on the bay the sun is glinting on the smooth ice and the pools of melt-water. There is a distant black spot, perhaps several. You know it's a seal, an Utuk, sunning itself by the blow hole. Seals have the same basic urge as the rest of us. If you have field glasses you can see its head come up and warily scan all around before it lies flat again.

You talk to your Inuit companion and decide who is to stay with the dogteam. He gets the draw and puts on a white cap to complement his white silopak. A pulled up hood would obscure his vision. Over his boots he pulls on a pair of white canvas socks. Next he takes two sticks, tied in the middle to make an X, and over the ends he fits a white screen — behold the Telluk.

Before the coming of the Hudson's Bay Company and other traders, there was no canvas, calico or similar fabrics. The Inuit made their telluks of sealskin. After the skins were properly cleaned they were soaked in urine; a common tanning process. They were next put out to bleach in the frost. The end result was a snow white screen. Of course white canvas or calico is easier to use and these man-made skins were quickly adapted to ancient techniques.

Now the Inuit is ready, rifle in hand, clad and screened in white. Only half a mile separates him from the seal. Sharp eyes have counted the sequence. Every so many seconds the Utuk raises its head, scans the bay ice, and settles down again.

As you watch the Inuit move toward the seal, he is counting the seconds, perfectly still just before its head comes up and moving quickly when it goes down. To the Utuk he is just another blob of ice in that vast expanse. You admire the skill and wish you could do it as well.

It takes a long time; stopping, counting, moving — stopping, counting, moving. Never do his eyes cease peering at the seal through the slit in the Telluk. You sit comfortably on the komatik, talking to the dogs and enjoying the sun on your face after the long winter. You hope that his concentration on the seal won't cause your companion to miss other blow holes where a seal might come up. You remember such times when a seal came up behind you and startled the daylights out of you, and your quarry.

Your friend seems near enough and you think he should

chance a shot. Then you realize his perspective is better than yours. You glance around and, bang, he has dropped the Telluk and is running for the seal. Fortunately, he grabs it before that submarine-like body slips down the incline to the hole. Many a seal is lost that way.

Sometimes when I'm bored or nostalgic I look at my Telluk and other gear. Will I ever get the chance to use it again? With the law as it is, thousands of Newfoundlanders and Labradorians can never get a license to hunt seal. It doesn't matter what the method or purpose. Isn't the seal legitimate game and food within the framework of fair and reasonable management?

Look at it the Inuit way in terms of technique, skill, patience, good health and culture. It's part of our culture too, whether we hunt with a Telluk or from a boat amongst the ice pans. There is nothing exclusively ethnic about it.

A SUMMER CHRISTMAS

There is nothing strange about a summer Christmas; ask any Australian, or anyone who celebrates the birth of Christ in the southern hemisphere. They don't even dream of a white Christmas; why would they if they have never seen one? People are adaptable animals and the same events mean different things to different people.

I remember one of my many Christmases away from home. It was my first year in Nain, and I was not quite twenty years old. I was single, of course but even if I had been married it would have been the same; though not quite as lonely.

The last boat sailed south on October 15th. My winter rations were stored and the wood was cut and piled for the winter. I got my first pair of sealskin boots, but didn't know they were mukluks until I heard Wilf Carter sing about them on the store manager's radio. Unfortunately, I didn't have a radio that first winter. Aunt Selma Voisey made my duffel parka with a khaki drill shuck. That was after I bought the famous bearskin Koulitak.*

It was a busy time that early fall and winter. Boat patrols were made before freeze-up and there were many things to learn about the people and the district, and about being the lone Newfoundland Ranger in the north. I didn't have time to be lonely until freeze-up. That was the period, like the spring break-up, when no one could travel except overland in their own locality. Isolation became a reality.

After freeze-up, travel began around the district but, except for some unusual emergency, we would not see anyone

---

* see chapter 3, page 107

from 'outside' until late spring or early summer. Dogteams were coming and going from around the bays and each arrival and departure was an event.

As Christmas Day drew near, I began to wonder how I could cope with it. The Government store had only staple foods and no luxuries, even in the drygoods section. I managed to find small items for Hayward and Selma Haynes, the store manager and his wife, and Henry Lyall, the interpreter. We had all become good friends.

On Christmas Eve there was a tree, and some cheer which Selma had carefully hidden away after the boat left. We had a nice evening and I was invited back for Christmas dinner. What a relief for a hungry growing boy; at last I was spared from my own novice cooking efforts.

On Christmas morning everybody in Nain went to the Moravian church, even me. There were friendly handshakes all around and the singing, all in Eskimo (now Inuktitut), was typical of anywhere in its sound. If you closed your eyes you could be anywhere.

The Band played in the afternoon, interrupted only when the odd instrument froze up. The Nain Band was a marvel under any conditions.

There was no turkey, no exotic vegetables, no cranberry sauce; none was available anywhere. But what a scrumptious meal Selma Haynes made of Canada goose, salt beef, turnip, potatoes and a huge delicious pudding. No meal could have been better prepared, or more generously offered to a lonely kid in strange surroundings. Later we visited around, particularly the missionaries; the Hettesch's and Peacock's homes. The goodies were plentiful and the hospitality genuine. The only thing lacking was family and childhood friends.

I think that at Christmas, of all times in the year, the ties that bind families pull stronger, and the strain of that pulling hurts a bit. There was nothing from home, but I knew that when the last mail was delivered in October.

That winter I learned a lot about myself and the people of

Northern Labrador. Travelling by dogteam from Nain to Zoar, Kamarsuk, Voisey's Bay, Sangu, Davis Inlet and Flower's Bay; and north to Webb's Bay, Black Island, Evilik, Port Manvers and across the Kiglapiat Mountains to Nutak and Hebron was a real experience. In one blizzard I came to realize that in the universal scheme of things I was no more important than a snowflake being driven before the wind. The cold, stark winter scenes, and the warmth and kindness of the people will burn in my memory as long as I live.

Finally spring came; you could strip to the waist and sunbathe in the middle of the day when travelling by dogteam. Partridge were out in their plumage and the long strings of geese could be seen and heard. By now, as much as I longed for the first boat, I almost dreaded its coming.

The ice moved out of Nain harbour on the 29th of June and the first boat in was the *St. Barbe*, the Magistrate's boat. We went down to the wharf as she steamed in. Everybody who normally got mail was waiting in anticipation. Magistrate Noseworthy, like some self-centred judges, had declined to accept liability for bringing the mail from Hopedale, where the S.S. *Kyle* had dropped it.

Nain from harbour ice, 1946

A few days later, we spotted the M/V *Winnifred Lee*, last seen on October 15th the previous year. All hands went aboard to socialize with Captain Josh Windsor and his crew. I came ashore with three bags of mail; most of it official.

I took out the letters and lined them up in date sequence, as shown on the postmark. It was necessary to read all that news as it unfolded. There were parcels too, Christmas parcels, which I eagerly opened. My dear old mother, God rest her soul, didn't realize the boats stopped running in October.

One parcel was obviously a Christmas cake. When opened, I was able to distinguish it under the mould. That cake sat on my kitchen table for several days before I had the heart to throw it out to the dogs; don't know if they ate it or not.

I had Christmas twice; once in December and again in July. Not many are that fortunate.

What is Christmas all about? It is a celebration not exclusive to practising Christians. Some of the ceremony has been borrowed from pagan times. But the so-called pagans were human beings like us; with the same needs, the same feelings of loneliness and the same yearning for family and friends. The giving and receiving is more human than religious; do it while you can.

THE JUDGE

Amandus Noah was a well-known resident of the north coast of Labrador in the 1940s. He moved to Happy Valley in later years and worked on the United States Air Force Base at Goose Bay. When I first met him, during the winter of 1946-47, he lived a short distance from Nain with his brother, Edward, and his wife. I have forgotten his wife's name, but recall vividly that she spoke English extremely well; better than Amandus, and his brother. They were outcasts, having been banished from Nain, but came in occasionally to trade at the Government store and visit close friends.

As it was told to me, Mrs. Noah was from some place in the Arctic, possibly Pond Inlet, and had arrived in Labrador some years before. Nobody knew for sure, but it was believed that she had at one time worked as a servant for the Hudson's Bay Company. She may well have been what was known as a 'country wife' of some manager; which could account for her command of the English language. It was customary for the

Nain, 1946

Chief Joe and Mary Rich, Davis Inlet, Labrador, 1946

Company to transfer personnel all over the north, including Labrador. In fact, I met two retired managers whose wives were from the high arctic. History buffs may recall that the Government of Newfoundland bought the Hudson's Bay trading posts at Hebron, Nutak, Nain, Davis Inlet and Hopedale in 1941.

Missionaries all over the world wielded tremendous power in the early days, and the Moravian missionaries were no exception. When I arrived in Nain as a young Newfoundland Ranger, I soon learned who called the shots. About the only people who had any real independence there were the manager of the Government store, who was a former Hudson's Bay manager, and the Ranger. Everything and everybody else were dominated by the Missionaries. It was a paternalistic society, and those who broke the rules suffered sanctions. For example, shortly after I arrived in Nain I learned that there was a 9:00 p.m. curfew in the village. That was the Mission rule, sanctioned and enforced by the village

Moravian Garden, Nain, 1946

elders; most of whom were also officials of the congregation. Shortly after I arrived, I was asked by one of the missionaries to enforce the curfew. Since it had no basis in law, I refused.

Those who were deemed guilty of serious transgressions could be banished from the village; it was the Christian thing to do! Of course, the sentence was always announced when the culprits met with the village elders; but they were the enforcers and didn't actually make the rules. That type of punishment, when imposed after a legal trial, would be harsh enough; the early settlement of Australia should provide adequate proof. Imagine being banished in Northern Labrador, totally without neighbours or access to the amenities of life. Some would say that might is always right, and righteous might justifies any action.

For some time I really didn't know Amandus Noah's proper name; he was always referred to as 'the Judge.' Before getting into that, it might be helpful to explain how he got the name 'Noah.' In the early days, before the arrival of the missionaries, native people had only one name. That applies to all races and civilizations if you research their early history. For example; a man could be called Metik, the duck; or Tuktu, the caribou, because of his unique walk. It was nearly always a name which identified some characteristic or occupation, as well as the person.

When government became more involved, and the bureaucrats began to maintain proper records of births, marriages and deaths, it was deemed necessary to have both given and surnames. This problem was solved in Labrador simply by instructing people, through their elders in the villages, that they had to choose another name. Many, if not most, on baptism were given 'non-pagan' names. Since the earliest Moravian Missionaries were German; names like Amandus, Seigfried, Gottwald, Hans, Johannes, Helga and Selma were bestowed. Those given names survive to this day. The main problem was to find surnames which could be properly recorded. Given a choice, some adopted the names of Newfoundland fishermen who frequented the coast; this accounts for the Barbours, Fords, Dickers, Webbs, and many other families. Some took surnames from their own language such as Millik, Atsertata, Pamak, Nokosak, etc. Thus 'the Judge' had a German-given name and a biblical surname. It was probably as intelligent a selection process as any. The clergy were the registrars all over Newfoundland and Labrador, on behalf of government.

Why was he labelled 'the Judge?' Well, I have no personal knowledge of the matter, because it happened before my arrival in Nain. However, I have no reason to disbelieve the story as I heard it from many sources, and over a long period of time. Besides, everybody around Labrador called him 'the Judge' and I suspect that most people did not actually know his name. From my knowledge of, and contact with Amandus Noah, I am satisfied that he was a very intelligent person who really didn't fit into society at the time. He was not willing to let the missionaries, or anyone else, lead him around by the nose. Also, he didn't seem to be committed, or indeed suited, to making a living from hunting, trapping and fishing. Like many of us, before and since, he tried to live by his wits. In that society, at that time, opportunities were limited.

Amandus thought up a scheme which would preclude hard work. One fall, after the coastal boat and all the fishing schooners went south for the winter, he told people that the

Governor of Newfoundland had appointed him a Judge. To prove this, he produced an impressive certificate which he had secured on the S.S. *Kyle*. This was an embossed guarantee which people as old as me remember came out of a Quaker Oats box. Since the Government stores dispensed bulk rolled oats, and most people couldn't read or write, it was easy to deceive them. He was careful not to show it to the few who were literate. The result was that he freeloaded off the people in several villages all that winter. Alas; he was found out because, as is well quoted, "he couldn't fool all of the people all of the time."

From that time on, life became difficult for Amandus Noah, a.k.a. the Judge. It was suspected that he and his brother, Edward, shared the same wife; a grievous sin. The kangaroo court sentenced the Judge to banishment. It takes no great amount of imagination to understand why the Judge joined the many migrants from coastal Labrador to Goose Bay: it was the Mecca of the North. Such wealth as the Americans and Canadians brought was beyond anyone's wildest dreams. As a result Happy Valley sprung up on the banks of the Hamilton River, near the air base.

There are many who will be upset to learn that the name 'Happy Valley' was applied throughout English history to communities which sprung up near military bases. A notable example is the Happy Valley which sprang up adjacent to the British naval base at Hong Kong. It was a temporary, un-planned, community of civilian workers, merchants and oth-ers who derived their livelihood from the presence of the military establishment. Subsequently it was all called Hong Kong, including what is now known as Kowloon. To the credit of Uncle Johnnie Broomfield, Isaac Rich, Gilbert Saunders and others, Happy Valley pushed aside its stigma and became an organized and prosperous community.

In the postwar era, with the phase-down of the military after the Cold War, Happy Valley-Goose Bay became a properly incorporated municipality. Happy Valley itself was the first incorporated community, and its first mayor was a survivor of the Nazi concentration camps; Leon Cooper. I recall hearing him speak during the visit of Lieutenant Governor Fabian O'Dea in 1967. He was extremely proud of the democratic country in which a survivor of the death camps could be freely elected mayor of a large town. Mayor Cooper and the Judge had something in common; they had both been outcasts and victims of religious intolerance. It was only a question of degree, and both earned a living thereafter as a consequence of Goose Air Base.

The enterprising Judge soon acquired a residence of his own in Happy Valley. It became a recreation centre for unattached U.S. Air Force personnel and poker games were nearly always in progress. The Judge prospered and became a person to whom native persons from the north coast would come for advice and assistance. With his knowledge of English, his intelligence and personality, he soon acquired the polished manners of the Base Commanders. He knew everybody and was not shy in making whatever approaches were necessary for himself and his clients.

In 1965 I made a career change and returned to Labrador the following year as the Judge of the Provincial Court; there were now two judges in Happy Valley! It was not long before I renewed my acquaintance with Amandus Noah; for obvious reasons I never addressed him as 'the Judge.' He would frequently come to see me on behalf of a client saying, "How are you, Your Honour? So nice to see you again. I wonder if you might assist me on behalf of (so and so)?" On other occasions he appeared before me as a defendant charged with some minor offense; he never lost his manners, or his cool.

On one occasion he came with a person from the coast who spoke very little English. After the usual pleasantries, he explained that his client had a problem with Revenue Canada and he was being assessed for income earned in the United States. It transpired that the form for that taxation year had the following question, 'Have you worked outside of Canada?' The answer which had been given was "Yes, the United States."

Now I knew the person who accompanied the Judge and was certain that he had never been out of Labrador. He was employed on the United States Air Force Base, technically part of the United States under the leasing agreement. When this was confirmed, the Judge told me that he had exhausted every avenue in trying to get through to the bureaucracy, without success. He had come to me as a last resort on behalf of his client. Under normal circumstances I might have had no greater success with the bureaucrats, but it just happened that there was an official from the St. John's Income Tax Office in town, whom I knew. He came over and straightened the matter out; the reputations of both Judges were enhanced.

The Monday morning Provincial Court sessions nearly always resembled a zoo. Aside from the number of cases, there were several nationalities working on the Base or living in the area. It was necessary to have a roster of interpreters, since cases were normally heard in the language the defen-. dants — or witnesses — spoke, Nascopi (a Cree dialect), Inuktitut, French, German, or whatever. We were reasonably well organized and the necessary interpreters were nearly always on hand. The courtroom was usually filled to capacity since, in addition to those who had to be there, the night shift from the Base came in for their weekly sport.

Amandus Noah was a defendant one Monday morning, and his case was one of the last to be heard. Before he departed the police brought in an Inuit defendant, whose case was not scheduled, but who wanted the matter disposed of summarily. All the interpreters had departed so the prosecutor asked the Judge if he would interpret. Being a true professional, and seeing an opportunity to pay his fine, the Judge readily agreed providing I approved. I had no objection, in the circumstances, as I was certain Amandus would interpret with complete accuracy.

The case began, and proceeded smoothly to the point where I forgot Amandus was getting old and a bit deaf. At one point, after I said something, he turned and said with a broad smile, "Speak a little louder, friend."

Amandus Noah, the Judge and former outcast, was a successful person after he moved to Goose Bay. Like me, he retired and lived with his memories until he passed on. In another age and society, who knows what he might have become. His native and social intelligence far outstripped his contemporaries; all he needed was opportunity. He made his mark, and will not be forgotten.

CONSIDER THE SEAL

A large seal has just been harvested by an Inuit Telluk hunter. The Telluk is a white screen used by hunters for centuries as a means of sneaking up on a seal basking at its breathing hole in the ice. I use the term "harvested" advisedly because using 'killed' might offend the sensibilities of someone in British Columbia, or Europe, or wherever, who is just waiting for a cause. That opportune cause allows them the solicit tearjerk money to fight for it. They live well, dining on thick steaks, while wearing expensive leather shoes. Note that most of them espouse a cause that is remote from where they live and thus does not affect those who contribute. Does anyone recall protests about the slaughter of cattle in Britain during the controversy about the mad cow disease? Of course, animal rights people will say, those cows were a serious threat to people. So is over-fishing by Europeans which contributed to the cod moratorium. Thousands have been thrown out of work. Irresponsible people say "Let government find alternative employment." With unemployment levels at all time highs before these industries were shut down, where can anyone find alternatives? There are many legitimate environmental causes, but some people make a career out of generating causes. If reasonable people act reasonably and responsibly, a balance of interests can be struck.

The new species of hunter emerged since World War II using psychological propaganda telluks. They harvest their victims with media-slugs, rarely seeing their prey eye to eye. Their beaters carry cameras and microphones to flush the game and they bag the employed resource harvesters. The carcasses are hung in the walk-in freezers of unemployment insurance and welfare.

Blubber Yard, Nain, Labrador, 1940

Contrast that type with the real hunter, the family provider. He is not emotional, uncaring or wasteful; but uses his own resources, energy and skill to pick up his pay cheque; the seal.

What will he do with the seal? That requires serious thought. The skin is valuable, whether used locally or sold. If for sale it must be carefully removed, cleaned, laced on a frame and dried. It can become part of a coat or other useful item. If prices are down it can be used at home. Different species of seal will dictate both home and commercial use.

A properly prepared and untanned skin is waterproof. It might smell a bit, mind you, but everything has its own odour; even humans, as you may have noticed.

Take Inuit sealskin boots, mukluks, kamiks — call them what you will. Nobody has ever designed or made a more versatile boot. In Labrador, as in most of the north, these boots come to just below the knee, are gathered at the top and have a drawstring. The Moravian missionaries introduced a system whereby the colour of the braid used for drawstrings would tell you whether a male or female was married or single. In Greenland some boots extended to the thigh.

With lapped and puckered seams, sewn with sinew by a good bootmaker, these boots are completely waterproof. The sinew thread is made from the dried large back muscle of the caribou. Before the sealskin is sewn, it is soaked and later softened by chewing it during the sewing process. When wet, the sinew swells to fill the needle holes. A good bootmaker can produce a completely waterproof boot when untanned skins are used. Even snow-water, which is said to leak through boiler plate, won't penetrate it. Years ago, while travelling by dog-team in the spring, I've waded through ice water for days. The only time I got wet was when I stepped in a melt-hole and went over my boots.

The best bottoms are cut from the square-flipper seal with the grain of the hair flowing towards the heel. When shaved close it provides good traction. In recent years, with skills declining, some boots in craft-shops have the grain of the hair different on each boot. It's a sure way of doing an impromptu ballet. The leg is wide, providing air space insulation; the stiff skin causes the leg to stand.

Wear these boots with a couple of pairs of homespun socks and duffel vamps and they are good to forty below zero. You see, unlike stiff soled factory-made boots, the foot is flexible and in motion all the time, aiding circulation. The only care required is to stretch the boots nightly on a piece of wood shaped like the leaf of a car spring. They are put on different feet each morning; they last longer that way.

What if the skin is not required for sale, clothing or footwear? It makes rope that will last for more years than you would care to use it, unless the dogs chew it up.

The seal is built like a submarine, or vice versa. The hunter will decide what length of rope he wants, make two appropriately spaced circular cuts, slip his knife all around the fat under the skin, and slide the whole band over the rear part of the seal. When this circular band is cleaned, stretched and dried, a blade is rigged and a continuous line or rope of required size and length is cut. Other parts of the sealskin can be used for dog harness, mitts, bags, and patches. Small seal pelts, properly removed, have been used as luggage, vacuum-type packs for food and floats for hunting.

Seal fat was used to light many a household, as did that of the walrus and whale. Train oil* from whaling and sealing predated kerosene. Both have a myriad of uses in the modern world. The Basque whaling station in Red Bay, Labrador is a prime example of European use of the whale. There is no doubt in my mind that seals were also processed at Red Bay.

Take a chunk of seal fat and lay in anywhere, even with moderate heat, and the oil will run right out of it: what richness. It's good to eat too. When frozen and sliced it's just like watermelon; in looks, I mean. It has been determined that seal milk contains more than 50% butterfat. No wonder those little seal pups become adults so quickly.

You can't get at the meat till the skin is off. Obvious, isn't it? Ah, the meat! Pure, rich diet food; no cholesterol. Seal meat is dark in colour and has its own distinctive taste. You have to make sure to remove as much of the fat as possible. Seal liver can't be distinguished from calf liver. What mouth-watering thoughts arise of flipper pie, stew, roast, rack of ribs, and curried seal. As an old friend says, "You can easily 'require' a taste for it." After all, who was born slurping snails, oysters and other unmentionables.

What a challenge the seal presents! It is a total life-support system of itself, in a variety of ways. A natural, renewable resource providing satisfying jobs in harvesting, packaging, marketing, fashion and industrial design and a wholesome diet food to tempt the palates of the robust and the jaded.

The biggest challenge is to assert our right to harvest our resources responsibly, building on our skills, and not relying solely on timid governments to fight our battles for us. Take up the Telluk and outwit the propagandists.

---

* Oil derived from marine animals.

THE BOUNTY OF THE LAND

BEARS LEARN QUICKLY

Over the years I've spent a lot of time around Lower Brook, which flows into the Churchill River about twenty-five miles from Goose Bay. Like most things it's probably not the same anymore, but it used to be a good area to hunt ptarmigan and grouse and there were lots of pike at the run-out. I used to walk all over that country and saw lots of bear sign, but not face to face. There was one high sandy hump where bears had a well-beaten path to the top. From the droppings and scuff marks you could tell where they sat down to survey the surrounding area. I can see them now in my mind's eye looking, but mostly sampling the smells on the wind.

My father spent a lifetime in the woods and never knew of one occasion when a black bear attacked a human. I've seen many bears before and since Lower Brook but never had reason to fear them. They can, however, be a great nuisance and destructive to property.

For many years I've played around with outdoor gear, modifying some and designing more. You never know if it works until it's field tested. Quite a bit of poor gear is designed by weekend sportsmen and sold by clerks who wouldn't find their way back if they stepped off the trail to relieve themselves.

Anyway, I had modified one of my tents by sewing a piece of canvas on either side of the canopy. The idea was to have a cooking shelter when it rained. Being anxious to try it out, I drove to Lower Brook over what was then known as the 'freedom road.' It didn't really go anywhere except in the general direction of Churchill Falls, but it was the longest piece of (forgive me) road going anywhere from Goose Bay.

It was spring — for up there — and I pitched the tent just

Bad weather cook shelter

off the road in a small gravel pit overlooking the brook. After everything was set for the night, I walked up Lower Brook and caught a few nice trout for breakfast.

Just before dark I cooked a steak and onions on the camp stove, sitting comfortably under the canopy in my folding chair. While I've camped rough, and still do, I like to be reasonably comfortable when possible.

It was a beautiful evening, with a light wind, and the combined sounds of the woods and brook made me feel quite content. I sat there for a long time and let my mind drift around.

As it usually happens in the clean, fresh air, drowsiness descended upon me. Trying hard not to wake myself up I crawled into the sleeping bag. The unwashed frying pan was left on the stove under the canopy.

Sometime in the night the tent collapsed. It is quite startling to be sleeping peacefully when the tent falls on you. Having a flashlight next to my head, I crawled out. There was no wind, so the tent couldn't have blown down, and I didn't see or hear anything. Anyway, I put the tent back up and hammered in the pegs securely. It was one of those umbrella tents with the centre pole. With the tent up, I checked around with the light and discovered several muddy paw marks on the white canvas which I used to modify the tent.

There was no mistaking the bear paw prints, so I flashed the light all around. Behold, there were two bears just a few yards away. Now don't take me wrong, I'm not that brave, but I was sure the bears wouldn't attack. After letting fly a few rocks, I was pleased to hear the bears taking off through the bush.

It was obvious they had smelled the steak and onions and, while sniffing along, one bear had fallen on the tent. He probably got quite a fright. I didn't because I was unaware of the cause at the time. Back to bed I went, after lighting a candle in the tent and putting the stove and frying pan in my vehicle.

After a long while I went to sleep again but was awakened by a series of grunts. I suppose they were asking each other where the food had gone. With some speed I got out of the sleeping bag and peered out through the screen door. There was Mr. Bear looking in. I let out a shout sufficient to frighten him, and me, and he turned and ran. This time I threw rocks in every direction, and went up from the gravel pit and cut a couple of dry sticks for a fire. When you spend a lot of time in the woods, especially in winter, spotting good firewood is almost automatic. Any good outdoors person will interrupt the most interesting conversation to observe, "there's a nice dry one."

With the fire blazing brightly in front of the tent, and the ends of the long sticks under the canopy, I finally went to sleep again. Twice in the night I woke up, reached out and pushed the ends of the sticks so as to keep the fire going; no more problems that night.

In the morning, after a good breakfast of trout, I was sitting back drinking good boiled coffee. Out came momma and pappa bear on the other side of the gravel pit. I guess they liked fried trout also. With the addition of a few dry stumps, the fire was still burning and I sat back and watched them. After a while they disappeared.

Yes, I know bears learn quickly. I wonder do we?

FROM TERRA NOVA BY CANOE

From Terra Nova, near the National Park; to Pool's Cove, Fortune Bay, Newfoundland. It's a long way to Fortune Bay; about one hundred and fifty miles as the canoe paddles, tracks, portages, shoots, lines, is swept off on its own. You have to be half cracked to think about it; to say nothing about actually going. Who would think about it except those driven by the knowledge that in a few years they will only be able to read about it; just like some of you.

The Goal

Every trip must have a purpose and we had several goals. We wanted to see the interior of Newfoundland, fish, try out a few new techniques, but mainly we wanted to climb Mount Sylvester. In 1822 William Epps Cormack and his guide walked across Newfoundland. He called the mountain 'Sylvester' after his Micmac guide. It's only 1234 feet high, but dominates all that interior area. Ray Zinck and I planned that trip a long time ago.

Ray planned and organized the food, packs and incidental gear. I provided a seventeen-foot Grumman canoe, tent and other camping gear. We have this down to a science; having been at it for years. Most of our gear has been so modified that the original manufacturers wouldn't recognize it; or we designed and made it ourselves. Except for the food, everything is light, portable and necessary. You wouldn't find our clothing in a slick catalog. Most people would be embarrassed to wear it, but it provides the workable comfort to get you there. As for food; we've tried all that space, and other, age stuff. The end result is normal, nourishing, tasty stuff;

supplemented by what we catch. Heavy? Yes, but worth it. Our menu? 'Eat something heavy, every day.'

Up the River

Some people have done this before; mostly the northern route via Rainy Lake. They usually fly in their gear to Kaegudeck or Jubilee Lakes. Everything is down hill when you get there: take a look at the map. We positioned the truck equipped for carrying the canoe at Pool's Cove. Ray's camper was placed at Eight Mile Bridge, just above Terra Nova. Four moose and one caribou were seen during that phase of the journey.

We left the Bridge at 1:55 p.m., July 28, 1985, pushing current all the way and spending a long time tracking the loaded canoe up through the rapids on a long line, or walking it. Did you ever try walking against a big river, water to your thighs, hour after hour? It is better for the legs than jogging, because the river bottom is not as smooth as pavement. A magnificent bull moose swam across a big steady and stood dripping glistening water in the sun, just to show us how easy it was. Mr. Beaver proved later it was easier than that. We

Ready to move — July 1985

51

camped at 9:45 p.m. on the edge of a rapid. After cooking a feed, we ate it with tired contentment. The moon played hide and seek through the silver birches across the river. I don't recall having much trouble sleeping.

Dangerous? My Eye!

While I'm not very literate, I read water. That is an academic skill necessary to canoeists. Sometimes I don't read very well, as subsequent events will show. However, going upstream or down, it is frequently necessary to scout ahead and read the water. When I came back from finding the best route through the rapids, Ray was holding the loaded canoe and squirming around the river. His foot was caught between two jagged rocks. He couldn't get clear without letting go of the canoe; it's a matter of balance. I held the canoe while he hauled his foot out of the boot. The collapsed boot came free: a lesson for when you are alone!

Late that evening we were lining the canoe up through a big run. To do this one holds the bow of the canoe in the current, while the other moves up along shore with a long rope to haul the canoe through. From time-to-time you

July 1985

52

change places to conserve energy; it sounds easy. In the process of keeping the bow straight until Ray could begin the haul, I slipped and struck my right eye on the bow of the canoe. For a moment, I thought I'd become a Cyclops. We talked about going back, but I still had one good eye. After a few days it cleared up, except for a huge bag of blood hanging underneath. It was just another bag to carry, and there was no one to be concerned about my looks. That night we made it to the old dam at the foot of Mollyguajeck Lake and camped.

And so we went on to Lake St. John, crossing early one morning before the wind came up. It was beautiful, even seeing it with one eye. Part of the way up the brook leading to Kepenkeck Lake, we ran out of water, or nearly so. We had to resort to moving rocks here and there to make a channel. The alternative was portage, portage, portage; how tired you get just thinking of it! At last we came across the remains of the old Anglo-Nfld. Development Company bridge, which crossed the brook en route to the remains of their last abandoned logging camp on Kepenkeck Lake. After a reflective lunch, we concluded it might be better to portage the two miles along the old road rather than continue up that waterless brook. That portage would mean seven trips each, including half of the canoe. It seemed enough to discourage even young people like you, wouldn't you say?

Surprise

Ray decided to walk a pack through while I was unloading the canoe. What a jolt he got on spotting two trikes outside a cabin, near Kepenkeck. He knocked on the door and a voice said, "Come in." It was a double shock to the occupants, as they thought their young companion was outside playing tricks. There were three Veys, Jack, Fred and young Perry. Thanks to their generosity, all our gear was transported across to the lake. Just think of all that effort on our part; suddenly rendered unnecessary. But for the reflective lunch at the bridge, we might have struggled up the other way.

Those good outdoors men will never realize what a favour they did. How pleasant to have a good chat after several days. Conversation is limited on the river; most discussion is inside your head.

That night we stayed in an old abandoned shed, near the derelict sawmill. It was more roomy than a tent; but not as clean, or flyproof. After several days of clean air, river music and running water for cooking and bathing, there is something obscene about broken down shacks, sawdust banks, slabs and rusting machinery. Thank all gods it was the end of the logging country; though nobody but a logger's son knows how important the forest industry is in Newfoundland.

Mount Sylvester

From Kepenkeck to Mount Sylvester the going is rough; small streams, ponds and portages. At times we had to work like dogs; past, not present day, dogs. Our last campsite before Sylvester was on the shore of a small lake. We set up in driving rain and wind; soaked to the skin and beyond, if that's possible. The next day we made two portages before breakfast. The final portage was through thick woods and swamp, or several combinations thereof. There was a bit of comic relief when, portaging through thick woods, the canoe jammed. We walked out from under it, and collapsed with exhaustion and hysterical laughter. The canoe stayed bottom up, about five feet off the ground.

The last part of that portage was along a caribou trail. It was worn waist deep in the bog by the passage of thousands of caribou, over time. There was Mount Sylvester, glimpsed occasionally through the driving mist and rain, across the next lake. We crossed and camped under it; grateful for hot brandy and good food. Cormack saw it from the same angle; in good weather, we hoped. It took us seven days of travel; did he do as well?

You have to attend to the practical things, such as drying out. August 3rd was beautiful — the mountain clearly seen

The Cairn on Mount Sylvester

against the sky. On the way up the long slope was one of the biggest bull moose we ever saw. We felt almost guilty invading his territory. From the top, the country spread out in all directions and we confirmed our route for the next day.

The Cave

There is a cave under the lip of Mount Sylvester. Cormack is said to have placed a can or bottle there with their names in it. We didn't find it; perhaps because the cave is badly eroded since 1822. But there is a mystery attached to that cave, so we discovered. Since you may not get there yourself, I'll explain as much as I can. In that cave there is a hand-carved memorial to Nonosbawsut, husband of Demasduit, (also known as Mary March after the month in which she was captured). Nonosbawsut was killed while trying to prevent her capture.

What a feeling, to reach your goal at an age when you wondered about your ability to do it; to bathe in the lake under the mountain and eat a good feed and fall into a dreamless sleep; like Cormack and Sylvester 163 before us. Who needs the unreality of dreams?

There are three long portages from the mountain, across Diamond Lake, before reaching passable water flowing into Kaegudeck Lake. It's all down hill from Diamond Lake; no more pushing current; just trying not to be controlled by it. Because of our appetites, we were now down to five carries each, plus half the canoe, on long portages. I'm not as tough as Zinck, and fell asleep on the night of August 4th while zipping up my sleeping bag.

Kaegudeck Lodge

We saw lots of moose and caribou, and entered a mirror-calm Kaegudeck. The lake is big, and the islands and shore loomed up. As an old friend is fond of saying, "it's just like scenery!" Across the lake we could see part of Kaegudeck Lodge on the skyline. That was overflow sleeping quarters, some distance up the hill from the lodge. The original lodge was built by Ches Crosbie, John Crosbie's father, in the 1950s. It is a work of imagination and heart; created by a man with a soul. After all those years there is not a sign of rot and the logs are perfectly preserved, inside and out. We were made welcome there, in the midst of the wilderness; wined, dined, showered

Caribou at Kaegadeuk Lake, 1985

and laundered. We slept in real beds too. Cormack never had it so good!

In the morning we waited until the guests went fishing. We had a good breakfast, bummed two steaks and two huge loaves of bread, and departed. Our host told us it would not be difficult descending the river into Jubilee Lake. It's obvious now that they had never done it, and we learned long ago never to trust Canadian maps of this Province. That river is continuous rapids and falls, with a few steadies in between. It was necessary to portage, and line, the canoe down as the river narrowed and the banks rose steeply.

Swamped

We scouted the river, reading the water and liking it less and less. At one point we decided to lighten the load and Ray carried a pack forward, moving roughly parallel to the river. When he came back, he reported finding a shack at the run-in at Jubilee Lake, but that the portaging was terrible. I knew the river banks were steep and the water fast and rock-strewn. We shot the canoe through one run, after tying the stern line to a tree. The next one looked worse, and I misread the water.

Zinck with a "light" load

There was a very narrow chute, and falls, with a big rock in the middle. About every third or fourth wave, the water would pile up against this rock. However, I felt the canoe would curl around the rock, unless the pile-up went in over the stern, when it dropped below the falls. It was a calculated risk and unfortunately I didn't tie the rope to a tree, as is wise in those circumstances.

As the loaded canoe shot out, and the stern dropped, it failed to curl around the rock and a big wave went in over the stern. A D-8 tractor couldn't hold it in the circumstances. Zinck hung on and I scrambled around the cliff hoping the free-floating bow line would swing in. The canoe swung out into the main tide and the rope was torn from his hands. It was a sickening feeling to see the canoe, with nearly all we possessed, over-ending and smashing its way down the rapids; it was my fault!

We clawed our way along the cliffs and found the canoe in the river, above another falls. It was jammed, bottom up, between two boulders. One paddle was stuck upright in a crevice, vibrating in the current. Zinck waded out along the canoe and cut loose two no-longer-waterproof bags; and the kitchen bag containing the stove, gas and utensils. The stove was an Optius 8R, which measures about 6x6x4 inches and burns a minimal amount of gas. My old pot, a veteran of countless trips, was tied under the front seat. The cover was tied on with rabbit wire; miraculously it was still in place. That pot still contained a pound of soaked beans, and two wet steaks from Kaegudeck Lodge. As Ray tied a line around these salvaged items, I hauled them ashore. We finally got the canoe ashore and hauled it part way up the cliff. After, we took the kitchen bag and pot and walked down to the shack at Jubilee Lake. Everything was gone and we calculated we were still ten days up country. There is not enough space here to describe how we felt; we, the veterans of all types of wilderness travel.

There were four bunks and mattresses in that shack. We

were soaked, discouraged and beat; but we cooked those two steaks and went to bed. After taking a mattress off each of two bunks, we placed them on the other two. Have you ever tried sleeping between two mattresses? It is fine until you turn over. August 6th, 1985, a memorable day!

Recovery

We got up at the crack of dawn; in fact, we were waiting patiently between the mattresses for it to crack. It was decided to search the river, each taking a side. Before long we found Zinck's main pack containing his sleeping bag and personal gear. It had floated down the river and hung on a shoal near the mouth. Next was an orange Rec-Pac, really a plastic knapsack, containing light foods. The current must have been too swift for it to sink. Nearly everything in it was soaked; we spread out the tea bags and everything else to dry.

After combing that river all morning, we recovered everything but two salmon rods, and our main packboard with the heavy foods. We strained our eyes searching every pool in the river but could not find it; short rations in the days ahead! After hauling the canoe up over the cliffs, we portaged it the last mile or so down through the woods to the lake. The main ribs were sprung, pulling the rivets out; the middle thwart was broken off; the sides were bulged and twisted, and there was a big hole in the stern. Only a Grumman canoe could survive such punishment. Fortunately, we caught enough trout for supper, to lessen the pain.

August 8th, was a hot day; great for drying soggy gear. We wired an alder across the main thwart. Ray closed the hole in the stern as much as possible, using a rock and a small pair of vice-grips from his pack. While the seams were being caulked with cotton-batting from the first aid kit, I went up on the roof and cut off as many blobs of tar as possible. Years ago we patched canvas canoes by running pitch into the cracks. When boiled in a can and poured into the cracks and holes, that tar did the trick. We calculated that bailing would only be necessary every half hour. So we loaded up and paddled across Jubilee and into Koskaecodde Lake, and camped for the night. From Koskaecodde, through Medonnegonix Lake and into the Bay du Nord River we went with the cripple canoe. We nursed it through the many rapids, frequently shooting it empty on a long line. On Thursday (not Friday) the 13th, we did six portages, and nursed the canoe through lots of rapids. Now we were down to one meal a day; in the evening. I remember that night Zinck was blowing up his air mattress. Because the tent was so small his habit was to lie under the mattress during this exercise. He woke next morning with the airless mattress still over him.

Finally we came upon better water and ran rapids continuously. We met the Hancocks and the Miles just above the last falls on the Bay du Nord, near the tidal water. They thought we were Indians; who knows? Before portaging around the falls we ate the last of our food; a cup-of-soup envelope and a cake of hard bread. You can appreciate the fact that we were still hungry. The Hancocks invited us to their cabin below the falls, where we devoured all their roast beef. Wilfred and Mrs. Miles towed us across the Bay into Pool's Cove. We loaded all our scruffy gear aboard the truck and left for Terra Nova; not to start all over again but to pick up Zinck's camper.

I was eleven pounds lighter in weight, and a little bit wiser when I arrived home. You see, in the last days we had nothing heavy left to eat.

It is highly probable that another long trip will take place. The music of the river, the flash of the paddle, the call of the loon and the tug of the salmon, surge strength into those aging muscles. There are many portages yet before I begin the long one!

TRACKING

In early August 1987 I got restless waiting for the Department of Fisheries and Oceans to re-open the salmon rivers. It was a dry summer and the water levels were down. My better half was away and I thought that if the four walls were about to close in on me, they might as well be tent walls. Loading the canoe, I headed up through Peak Pond, Split Rock and Old Sea to the head waters of the Salmonier River on the Avalon. No, I didn't forget to secure that all important Wilderness Area Travel Permit.

It was hot and dry and, except for the fact there was no fishing, a very pleasant trip indeed. If you asked me about the portages, it would be difficult to reply, "No sweat" but the canoeing was superb and I would recommend it to any reasonably robust person. It's true wilderness, and fairly close to what we term 'civilization.' The starting point is Peak Pond, less than a hundred yards off the highway and less than an hour from St. John's.

Up country, the water was low and warm but even when you can't fish, it's really something to see and hear the salmon splashing and flopping around. It was easier to take lying down in the sun with not a soul around to disturb your thoughts, or sitting in front of the tent as the sun sets over the water and behind the rolling barrens.

The beauty of canoeing solo is that the only things to distract you are what you want to see and hear. One day the wind was calm and I paddled up to a mother duck and her six ducklings. Another time, while having lunch, I spotted a stag caribou on a nearby island. After paddling down around and stalking him, I managed to get two good pictures; one looking at me and the other while swimming away. How often

I wished I had a good telephoto lens and the technical skills of a good photographer. It is possible to get quite close to some wildlife, but they always look a lot smaller when you get the prints back. On the way back home I camped on a high barren point on the shore of Old Sea. It was necessary to store up enough energy for that long, final portage the next day. As I discovered the next morning, it was a bit to close to an ant hill. However, they go to bed at night too and only bother you in the morning.

I got up with the ants. It was a beautiful day; Old Sea was pacific. The sun was bright and warm, not a black fly to be seen, heard or felt. There were few flies that summer. Being alone in the world, I peeled off what scant clothing there was and had a good bath. It's usual to do this in the evening before collapsing in sleep. When your only toilet articles are a bandanna and a piece of Sunlight soap tied in the toe of the spouse's nylon sockette with a clip on the end, it's easier to dry off naturally. Conditions were right that morning. The coffee was already boiling so I sat down in my legless chair, which also serves as a pack-board, and put together a sumptuous breakfast. It was pleasant being just another animal in the wilderness, wearing only his skin.

Since there was only one more portage, all day to do it and no one to push me, I spent a long time over breakfast and coffee. Where I sat was right at the clear water's edge where the bank fell sharply away to a deep hole. Small trout were moving around feeding, so I used to flick out the odd crumb and watch them play water polo with it. It was really peaceful sitting there with only the odd inquisitive blue-reared fly or ant landing or crawling over places not usually accessible.

Most people rarely admit that they are not always consciously and purposefully thinking. I'm old enough to be an exception and just let the old mind wander where it will, especially in such pleasant and free surroundings. Soon I realized I was doing a mental scan of the trip, up and back.

Then I was thinking about Louis L'Amour's book, 'Last of the Breed.' The mind is the original computer, capable of scanning in the passive periods without a programmer or operator.

The 'Last of the Breed' is about a mixed blood Sioux Indian and a Siberian Yakut; both having the highly developed skills of their ancestors, particularly in tracking. The setting is Siberia and the hunter-tracker is the Yakut, while the quarry is the Sioux. It's a fantastic story about ancient skills, modern politics and geography. There is much to learn from it.

Tracking game requires highly developed skills; how much more so before the invention of field glasses, guns, boats and aircraft. It required a knowledge of fish, animals and birds and their relationship to weather, seasons, habitat and a host of other things. A few years ago a friend of mine was tracking a moose through snow. On hearing a noise, he thought the moose was doubling back. At the ready, he saw another fellow emerge from the woods, tracking the moose backwards; what skill!

Man-tracking was an important skill in frontier days, and still is in those countries plagued by rebel warfare. Both the tracker and the quarry needed almost equal skill; the one to stalk and the other to evade. The sign was minimal and required sharp eyes, ears, nose and perhaps that rare quality known as a 'sixth sense.'

That is not so anymore, especially in North America. These days any fool can follow human tracks. The real problem is to determine who, how many and when they left that well marked trail. You can track them in the city from the store where they bought the bar, chips or cigarettes along to where they threw the wrapper down while passing the garbage receptacle placed there at the taxpayers expense. From the fast food outlets to Signal Hill, Bowring Park and the shopping malls all over the province where the boxes, cups, bones, mustard, catsup and God-knows what fell away from the car windows. Unfortunately the pigeons, crows, gulls, and roaming dogs can't eat the boxes, bottles and plastic utensils. You can track our 'pampered' citizens along the highways by following the white and yellow blobs splattered on the pavement. It must be to show the foreign tourists how 'effluent' we are. Our provincial symbol should be a gravel pit with overflowing garbage bags on one side, a car wreck on the other; with a forested background which looks like a war zone.

Now, it is like that in highly visible places, where the droppers don't have to carry their garbage tracks to easily accessible organized places of disposal; how easy do you think it is to track them over the portages, along the rivers, and through the winding ATV trails?

From the Salmonier highway where you put your canoe into Peak Pond and until you paddle offshore, there is a trail of beef buckets, beer bottles, pop cans, old socks, chip bags and Vienna sausage cans. I'd almost bet there are sausage cans on the moon, since I've seen them from Newfoundland to Alaska. At the end of the little canal flowing out of Peak Pond there is a sheet-plastic dam weighed down by rocks and backed by a haul-over for boats; an ingenious use of future garbage.

When you pick up the portage to Old Sea there is the same trail of bottles, cans, plastic containers and, strangely enough, the sole of one shoe. I've pondered this many times since without coming to a rational conclusion; some lost 'sole' I suppose.

Along the other portages and at the entry points for boats and canoes the same, or worse, conditions prevail. Around the convenient camping places it's compounded. At Metcalfe Falls; garbage, garbage, garbage. Someone even left their pants. They couldn't have been one jump ahead of the Fisheries Officer. There must be some other explanation for I've seen the same situation all over Newfoundland and Labrador, but I suspect some of you know. Potential garbage is heavy to carry into the wilderness but, with the deep bog holes and safe burning places, what remains is easy to carry out. If these were frontier days, those responsible would be easily tracked down and killed by marauders. Perhaps that punishment is a bit too harsh for the uncaring.

Some years ago, before the government closed the Swine Breeding station off Portugal Road near St. John's, I had occasion to visit. Though I didn't say anything, I felt a little insulted that all visitors had to strip, shower and put on sterile clothes in order to visit the pigs. However, on sober reflection I realize why unsanitary humans should never be allowed to visit the clean pigs.

BURPING A SALMON

Most people know about burping a baby, but I suspect there are few who know anything about burping a salmon. I discovered this process by accident. Now that fishermen are involved in the great 'catch and release' debate, it might be as good a time as any to let you in on this nearly secret process. I can't say it's really secret because I've told the story a number of times while having a pleasant tot with other fishermen. Some believed it, others did not. But then few people have had the opportunity and, fewer still, the inclination to test it. I even went so far as to write the management of the Department of Fisheries and Oceans in St. John's to outline the process, and express my views on the destructive policy of 'catch and release.' Some years have passed and I am still waiting for an acknowledgment; a rational reply would be out of the question.

Larry Butt, my brother-in-law, and I were camped on the Flower's River, near Davis Inlet a few years ago when the daily limit for salmon was eight. We were there for a full month with our tent set up on a big rock in the middle of the rapids. There were two reasons for the campsite, 1) it allowed us to fish for sea-run speckled trout when we were in the mood to have trout for breakfast and, 2) it protected our food and equipment from prowling black bears. We all know that bears can swim, if they want to, but like people, they don't want to exert themselves unnecessarily.

We had excellent fishing that summer as we moved up and down the rapids by canoe from our campsite. Now, you can only eat so much salmon, so we fished with barb-less fly hooks and released everything we couldn't eat. Larry has since passed on to the happy fishing ground. He was quite a fisherman, having learned well on the Upper Humber River. I've seen him hook, play and hold up a salmon to be photographed many times, using barb-less flies. Never have I seen another fisherman able to do it.

You may not believe it but salmon fishing on a river like the Flowers can actually be boring; catch and release, catch and release. I often quit fishing to watch mother goose herd her fluffy little goslings along the river bank. Other times I roamed up and down the river, checked over the gear, and generally killed time.

As you may know, most salmon are pretty sick when they are caught and for that reason I never use a gaff or net, just an old woollen glove. I hold them by the small section above the tail, head down, and they stay quite still.

One day I kept a salmon which had bumped itself around on the rocks before being landed. I thought it wouldn't live if released, and consequently kept it for supper. Shortly after I hooked another in the next pool, and the same thing happened. One salmon is more than enough for two people, so I patted that salmon on the head and let her go in the quiet, shallow water. She turned belly-up. I quietly reached in and held her upright in the water and that salmon stayed under my hand as quiet as a kitten. After a little while she gave a shudder, like hiccups, and a couple of bubbles of air came up from her gills. I let her go but that salmon turned belly-up again, so I held her in the same manner with my hand lightly on her back. After what seemed a long while, she burped again and more bubbles came up. I let her go but she made only a feeble thrust with her tail and turned belly-up again.

Now I became more interested and held her for what seemed like an eternity. She burped twice more, becoming a little more frisky each time. I'm not trying to say my humanitarian instincts were aroused because I still catch and kill salmon, but this was thought provoking. I've forgotten how many times that salmon burped, but the last time she swam away as lively as anything.

Over a supper of salmon, boiled with a piece of salt beef, I told Larry what had happened. Anyway, we decided to try it again on the next sick salmon we landed.

The following days we burped salmon and they swam off okay. We also tied sick salmon by the tails in a rock pool to see if they would actually survive the burping process. They were so lively next morning we had quite a tussle letting them go.

Well, I don't know what the scientific explanation is, but I think that those salmon take in oxygen from the air when they are jumping about with the fly in them. The normal process is to extract the oxygen from water through their gills. Exertion may be a factor, but there is a lot of exertion in travelling from the sea to the headwaters of the rivers. I believe that 'out of water' breathing by salmon equates with air embolism in humans. When oxygen is injected directly into the bloodstream in humans it can cause death, or at best extreme sickness. It seems possible that, if the salmon can keep its equilibrium, it will burp and recover. I have burped numerous salmon in the years since and have not known the process to fail.

With angling rules now changed, and 'catch and release' a requirement, this might be the answer to the survival of some of these noble fish. However, I just wonder how many fishermen have the interest, inclination, or the patience to burp their salmon. Before proceeding further I want to make it abundantly clear that, since the Flower's River trip, I have never deliberately caught and released fish. Whatever the daily limit may be; I catch that number, dismantle my rod and leave the river. I'm satisfied that, given the level of under-standing and lack of concern of most fishermen, the 'catch and release' policy is really 'catch and destroy.'

GOOD ENOUGH TO EAT

Trout River, Moose Management Zone 5, known to most hunters as Goose Arm, is prolific moose country. It is most accessible from Deer Lake, and comprises a large strip of territory roughly bounded by the Viking Highway, Gros Morne National Park, Deer Lake, the Humber River, Humber Arm and the Gulf of St Lawrence. It is crisscrossed by numerous miles of logging roads, which frame cut-overs, and must be as attractive to moose as Florida is to Newfoundlanders in winter. You can stand on the side of a ridge near Otter Pond, for example, and view the whole countryside; seeing moose frequently. Of course, most of them are too far off to shoot, but they are noble animals to watch. The stillness is broken only by the wind, crows calling across the valley and the odd ATV. How nice to get away from it all; you can almost forget the garbage on the bank of that nice clear stream that flows out of the hillside.

We had a license for either sex, unlike most hunters we met who had 'bull only.' I won't go into how we got our moose; suffice it to say it was a nice bull of about 500 pounds. (It irks me to say kilograms, or mention kill in any way, since there are sensitive people around.) Anyway, it was relatively easy, until the moose was down.

As we watched some hunters maul, mangle, drop and drag their moose from where they got it to their less than clean vehicles we began to wonder why they ever expended so much energy. Most of the meat looked as though a dog might reject it, if it were offered. Surely it couldn't be meant for food unless they meant to give it to their worst enemy.

Now, the Wildlife Department has taken a good first step in their Hunter Capability Courses. Also, the booklet which

Moose at Aidies Stream, November 1989

accompanies big game licenses is well put together, and they are to be commended for it. However, perhaps the inspection division of the Department of Health should be more actively involved with Wildlife Officers in hunter education and field monitoring. Discharging a firearm is only a part of hunting. Unfortunately, Wildlife Officers are so scarce that we didn't see one at all.

When considering how to clean the animal just downed, take all the expert advice you've been given and match it against two basic facts:

1. Bullets don't always hit where you want them to;
2. The animal is not downed in controlled conditions.

Almost in every occasion it's not a clean shot, and the spot where the animal goes down usually couldn't be more awkward if your worst enemy chose it. Thus, you have to accommodate the conditions imposed on you. If you are hunting solo the work really begins. It's messy and time consuming, but let's face it, you owe it to yourself and the animal to do the job properly. You have to endure the discomfort no matter what the weather.

The basic procedure is well laid out in the Hunter's Booklet, which I am sure is propped up near the moose and followed closely. There are five essential items, beside the obvious knife, which make the work more convenient and aid in doing a satisfying job.

1. Some string; I always carry the braided nylon type which is available at most fishery supply stores. It is as strong as a ship's cable, very light in weight and does not run dye.

2. A good sharpening stone: You'll have to touch up that Rambo knife several times.

3. A saw: Contrary to what is usually recommended, the best type is an old handsaw. You can cut it off to make it fit in the pack. Its width makes for straight cuts, and there is no frame to obstruct.

4. Rope: You'll need it for hanging the quarters. If you hunt alone a small pulley is helpful. It can be purchased locally at a reasonable cost.

5. Fishing, or trawler net. When this is cut to appropriate size two sticks can be reamed through, and you have a strong stretcher for carrying the quarters to the road.

My good spouse nicknamed me 'String' years ago because I can produce it from almost every pocket. It's the greatest thing since sliced bread and I wouldn't even begin describing the millions of uses. In moose hunting it can tie off the organ and the rear end, to avoid spillage. Also when the main intestine is to be cut, two pieces of string tied a knife blade apart, solve a lot of problems. Anyway we got our moose just before dark and he came down amongst some small trees. We juggled the animal on his back and tied out the four legs with string. It was after dark by the time it was cleaned. We put two sticks in place to keep the cavity open for cooling and went back to the tent. Needless to say, we marked the place. The night was cool so there was no reason to worry. We just had to be back there before the crows got up next morning.

The finished product, 1979 Goose Arm, Deer Lake

Most animals are quartered with the hide on to facilitate moving them to the nearest transportation. Many people bring them home that way and try to skin them in the garage, or whatever. Frequently the meat is contaminated, or if it isn't, certainly does not look too appealing. The best place to clean and skin the animal is in the woods; as close to a brook or waterhole as you can get. You can put a stout pole between two standing trees. In our case, thanks to Bowater's, there were no convenient standing trees. We made a tripod of smaller poles for each quarter.

When skinned, we trimmed off unwanted sections and washed the quarters with 'J' cloths dipped frequently in the brook. We then let them drain and crust and put on their gauze socks. When we hung those quarters in Norm White's coldroom in Deer Lake they looked as good as any found in the best meat market. Those beside them left a lot to be desired.

Not only was that moose excellent meat, but we had no hesitation in serving it to discriminating friends. So, we say to you hunters, "You got your moose, but can you eat it with relish?"

ARE YOU HUNGRY?

You must be hungry, if not you will be when I am finished. Walking, snowshoeing, snowmobiling, paddling or whatever always works up an appetite. If not, eat anyway purely out of habit; it's a nice pastime. When out in the woods alone, I never care how long it takes to cook supper; it's a time consuming ritual, with a reward at the end.

While camping, follow me through an eating day. I hope you get fed up half way through. What about breakfast? You get up early, about 5 a.m., mainly because your back hurts, you're cold, or you have more fluids than you can stand. Get up and hook the sleep out of the corners of your eyes; I'm getting breakfast in the winter tent. Perhaps you should stay in the sleeping bag for a few more minutes.

Breakfast

First; light the fire, with matches. None of this business of twirling a stick with a bow. I doubt if it works at forty below zero anyway. Matches are as aboriginal as the snowmobile, chainsaw, gun and the outboard motor. The kettle is boiling; heave in two filter packs of coffee. Let it boil and then set the kettle back; percolators and drip machines are just cosmetic. Taste the pure, strong boiled stuff for proof. "Couldn't swear to it, Your Honour, but I knows 'tis coffee." What do you want, bacon and eggs? (don't mind the little black specks, they're harmless). Baloney and eggs, or beans? Okay, it's yours. Toast? Stick two slices on the side of the camp stove. Why? Because the stove is small and the top full. When they smoke that side is done. Whack on the butter; never mind those green things, they're spruce needles. No more toast? It's not pop-up; it's burn-on and fall-off!

Bread is not easy to carry outdoors. The ready-sliced baker's stuff squeezes up in the pack: homemade is best. Get out your trusty knife; it's an Opinel, made in France and sharp as a razor. "You 'avent got an 'op-in-'el without one. Ask any Hinglish teacher from Hupper Hiland Cove, 'e'll know what I means. "On that note, we used to practice dropping our aitches when I went to school. The exercise went like this: — "It's not the 'eavy, 'eavy, 'auling what 'urts the 'orses 'ooves; it's the 'ammer, 'ammer, 'ammer on the 'ard 'iway what 'urts the 'orses 'ooves." Slice off more bread boy; mind that thumb!

Getting breakfast in the summer is a 'piece of cake.' You light up the Coleman or propane stove or, for me, an Optimus 8R, and juggle the pan and kettle; don't worry about the flies.

Lunch

Okay, you didn't die of indigestion, and hunger strikes again. The symptoms are universally recognized; they cross all races and cultures. Everybody is hungry, in every time zone; especially you.

Put on the kettle; have a cup-of-soup to keep you alive. While you are alternately blowing and slurping, I'll pop two Magic pantry beef stews in the kettle. They are meal size vacuum packed pouches which need no refrigeration. All you do is heat them up and eat them up. They're delicious and save a lot of time. There are several types of meals in this brand available in any supermarket. They beat freeze-dried foods, or those little cans of sausage. By the way, if you know anyone who has the secret of getting those little sausages out, just let me know.

If you want to top off the lunch, try Purity gingersnaps and Philadelphia cream cheese. Those little tubs, or cartons of cheese fit comfortably in your knapsack. What a desert; no mess, no special utensils! Wash it down with a couple mugs of tea, and have a good rest before you move on.

Supper

All afternoon on the rabbit trail, or any trail, causes the insides to speak again. What's for supper? Deer-fried-rice (or beef, or moose)? Sounds exotic eh? All the utensils you need, if by yourself, is a Teflon frying pan and cutlery. I always use stainless steel, including mugs. There is no elaborate washing that way; just boil the works in the frying pan after the meal. Plates are used when there's company; paper plates, if the meal is not sloppy. Just cube that deer steak and fry it in bacon fat or olive oil. The latter doesn't spit or splatter your immaculate surroundings. When the deer is well fried, slice in a couple of onions, cook and stir. Keep the heat up on your tent stove with well split wood; dry juniper is best. Smells good, what?

Flick in a little salt and pepper and 'where's your sister sauce.' Next, fill the frying pan with hot water from that singing kettle, and stir in a package of Oxo. What for? Well, wait and see! Now fill the pan with minute rice and sprinkle in another package of sauce, if you have one. Also, stir in an egg; unless it is frozen. Put an old plate, or kettle cover, or a piece of tin foil (neatly folded in your pack) over the pan and sit back. You can toast your feet, go outside for a gasp of cold air, or do whatever you like. After a few minutes that cover will rise off the frying pan; all the liquid is gone. Cooked, me son! Stir the deer-little-onions through and eat with a big spoon. Any rice you drop will fall on the stain master carpet; the boughs on the floor. Man! I'm full and will have to take a nap before having bread and jam, or bread and honey; or both, if you like.

Oh, yes; snacks are permitted between meals, if there's time.

Variety

There are endless varieties of good food suitable for camping. I try to ensure a balanced, interesting diet and at the same time keep the packs light in weight. Having gone the distance on super-light foods, I've gone back to more conventional packaging. It may be heavier, but it gets lighter after you eat it.

For breakfast there is pre-cooked and packaged rolled oats; instant porridge. That is very useful for rolling on fish before frying. Then there's the usual stuff, bacon, eggs, canned meats, etc. A large can of soup, spiked with a can of corned beef, makes a good lunch for two. On long canoe trips we cook a big meal in the evening. What is left over is placed in a clean plastic bag and put aside. We then have hash and coffee for breakfast; not exactly gourmet food, but nourishing. Only the frying pan and mugs need washing in the morning. Pancakes go down easy; we find that Bis-quix is best. All you have to do is throw in a few raisins, or blueberries in season, and you have a meal. On that note, once on a canoe trip in Labrador, we came across an abandoned house in Adlatok Bay with a large rhubarb patch in front. We cut and tied bundles and threw it in the bottom of the canoe. When we stopped for a break every five days, we had rhubarb jam. The only problem was, we had to drink our tea and coffee without sugar. Sweets are essential when you work hard.

The same Bis-quix makes an excellent pudding when tied up in a 'J'cloth and thrown in with the evening meal. Pale-face bisquits can also be made from it and baked in the pot. 'J' cloths are useful too for making peas pudding. The main advantage is that you avoid washing up.

Spaghetti and macaroni are good foods to work on. All pastas stick to your ribs; even hard bread, which can be eaten as is, or cooked in a variety of ways. Hard bread is pure, local, pasta; never discount the experience of sailors on long voyages. Dried beans, peas and rice will keep forever, if you keep them dry. If you're planning beans for supper, let them soak in the pot while you paddle. In the evening throw in whatever you can think about, and it's beans-plus.

I always carry onions (dried, if you like) and it doesn't matter if they freeze. Carrot and parsnip go well in stew, frozen or not. Eggs are okay frozen; they won't spoil that way. All you have to do is peel them, because the egg shrinks in the shell when frozen. To cook, just slice the eggs in half, lengthwise, and place them flat-side down in the pan. When fried you can't tell they were ever frozen. Small bottles of tabasco and 'where's your sister' sauce, and packages of Oxo envelopes will jazz up any meal. So will film containers of garlic, curry and chili, and they don't take up much room. Curried Newfoundland steak,* with rice, is excellent.

Living off the Country

Nobody does it for real; not even the aboriginals. Pickings were slim for them before the Hudson's Bay Company and the corner store. We haven't seen a lean aboriginal since. However the diet can be supplemented with game; in season, of course! What else would any law-abiding citizen say.

Rabbit, ptarmigan, grouse and even squirrel make excellent stew; especially when seasoned with the little goodies I mentioned. Not too many get a chance at moose liver and bacon.

Fish

Ah, Trout! I like them best filleted, even the small ones. You roll them in rolled oats or a little corn meal. A plastic drug bottle will hold enough of the latter. Fry them crisp in olive oil and you can pick them up in your fingers and munch away. They are also excellent cubed, and sprinkled with garlic power.

Salmon and char; now we are really getting exotic! You can fry it if you like, but nothing beats a couple of hunks of salmon or char boiled with a piece of salt beef; now that's a delicacy! On long trips when we don't have to bring the fish back to prove we caught them; we eat fish twice a day. It keeps us slim for portaging through the thick woods.

Saltwater fishing is very much a part of the outdoors-

* Baloney.

Planking a salmon, Adlatok River, Labrador, 1980

man's life. Jig a nice cod and strip his skin off before he knows it. Next, boil him in seawater with a piece of his liver about the size of your little finger nail. If you haven't tried it, you haven't lived. I'm writing this in English because if France finds out, they will want more of our fish.

Now don't get the idea that all we do outdoors is eat. It's just another of the joys of living. Tastes are keener and ceremony doesn't matter. I can even understand why, in some cultures, belching is a sign of appreciation.

The Result of Eating

Eating creates garbage. In fact, about two thirds of what we buy is, or becomes garbage. Cosmetic packaging is the culprit. In the wilderness it must be burned, stamped down in the deep bogs, or brought out; on your back if necessary, since you brought it in. I've travelled all over the Newfoundland and Labrador wilderness. There are many places I'll never see a second time, but you won't find my garbage there. I hope you won't leave any.

Now, after all that, are you hungry?

GIVE US THE TOOLS

There is no intention here to paraphrase the utterances of Winston Churchill. It is merely an attempt to indicate how outdoor gear can be modified and improved to make life a little more comfortable. Much of what is available on today's market is made of good materials, and some of the designs are superb. However, just like the super-sophisticated automobile, which will do everything including telling you when you are lost, some components just don't work. Why is it that, with all the engineering and technology available, windshield wipers just don't work properly? It may well be that the basic designs don't contemplate much rain or snow since the bulk of the world's population lives in warmer climates. Perhaps such a minor matter is beneath the intellectual dignity of major designers. At any rate, such things are a major nuisance under certain conditions. Why, even the car bodies are tapered towards the roof to allow rain and snow to fall in on the expensive seats! It appears there are many flaws covered by the concept of aerodynamics; as if cars could fly.

Quite a few years ago I was moose hunting solo in the Taylor's Brook area, near Deer Lake. It seems most things happened years ago; the penalty of creeping age I suppose. I had an old .303 calibre rifle without a sling in one hand and an ax in the other. While crossing a deep brook on a slippery log, I was forced to do the woodsman's ballet in order to avoid falling into the water.

Now the rifle was borrowed; hence no sling. The ax was mine and, like millions before me, I carried it in my hand.

That night, lying back in the open-front shelter with a fire reflecting mostly light, I got to thinking there must be a better way to carry an ax. You've all seen the belt ax with the sheath, and the big ax with sheaths of varying designs? They look good in the catalog, or store, but are not worth a tinker's curse in actual use.

Aside from dragging your pants off, the belt ax will pound your arms off and break your back while chopping wood for the night. As a carpenter's ax it is marvellous, but most outdoor types do their carpenter work at home.

The long-handled ax, with sheath, is equally awkward to carry. Sure the sheath protects the blade and you, but you either carry it in your hand or pack. In the pack the handle sticks up and becomes a nuisance, for the many reasons you can think of, and the sheath is always mislaid when the ax is in use.

Perhaps axes don't arouse much popular interest today, but one time everybody had at least one. We needed them for cutting wood, splitting kindling, and numerous other uses. Some of us still need them. If I ever had to choose one tool, out of the many now available, without hesitation I'd take the ax. It has multiple uses outdoors, even as a weapon, and ranks above the match as a basic survival tool.

A good quality, light-weight ax with a standard-length handle will last for many years with minimal care. One of my axes had a defective handle; it only lasted twelve years. The handle should be 'flattish' so that it won't twist over in your hands. Those nicely rounded handles look better, but are dangerous when iced-up or wet. A few inches of hockey tape, from the ax head back along the handle, will prevent splintering. By squirting blaze orange paint on the end you'll help avoid loss, especially in the snow.

Anyway, some of that firelight must have caused a flicker in my brain because, as they say, "like a bolt from the blue" the answer came. Before knapsacks or rucksacks became such, they were carried in the hand. Somewhere back in history, someone got fed up with that and put a sling on the bag. Next, they added two slings and 'presto,' we had the knapsack. Primitive style bags can still be made by placing a potato, or stone, in each of the bottom corners, tying a line around each and joining the two pieces to close the top. The advantage of using potatoes is that you can eat them. Just like the wheel, the knapsack was jazzed up over the years. But the wheel is still a wheel, or in this case a bag. Both these marvellous inventions were conceived by people without university degrees. It takes degree-types to design the decor.

So in my primitive way I thought, 'the bag went from hand to back, why not the ax?' It took a while to vary from the prototype, but the design is very simple. An old revolver holster is cut down; two 'D' rings are attached; a length of braided nylon rope is cut; the ends knotted or sewn to the 'D' rings; a cord-lock is slipped over the other end, or a small loop knotted in. Put the ax in the holster; put the strap across the head; slip the loop over the ax handle; pull the cord-lock tight and put the thing on your back like a knapsack. When your arms go through the rope it pulls the loop down the handle, and the ax will never come off on its own. The ax can be removed from your back, when necessary, without taking off the sheath. It protects the ax, you, and can be hung within sight or safely tied on the ATV, snowmobile or canoe. My buddies and I now carry our axes on our backs, alone or with a knapsack. Harken onto me you 'peaceniks;' turn revolver holsters into ax sheaths, and spears into walking sticks!

That crack is enough to make those peace loving people want to knife me. However, I bet they don't have knives efficient enough to do it. It used to be said that you weren't a Newfoundlander if you didn't have a knife. Almost everybody had a pocket knife in the old days, and in most cases it was an I.X.L. The pocket knife is still the best small all-around tool. I always carry one, except on airplanes. Unfortunately the designs are sometimes awkward, especially those with cork-screws, and they wear out the pockets in the best suits. Not many of us carry wine around every day, especially in the woods.

A simple little sheath, preferably of soft leather, co-ordinated to your suits, with velcro on the flap, will do the trick. On canoe trips I carry a double sheath, homemade, with a pocket knife, yachtsman's knife and a small sharpening stone. The spike on the second knife is very useful. A velcro flap will close itself, even if you forget it. Losing a knife outdoors can be dangerous, as well as expensive.

I have to be a bit delicate about this; but it is a common problem when carrying knives. If you attach a nylon string loop to your knife sheath, no matter what kind of a knife you carry, and thread it around a belt loop, it will prevent loss. It also avoids nasty-nasty situations when you have to undo your belt outdoors. Invariably the belt will slip through the loops, including that on your knife sheath. The weight of the knives aids in slippage. Bodily functions are just as frequent, and perhaps more regular, when you are in good health and getting lots of exercise: so much for the 'bare' facts!

There are all kinds of little twists to make life a little easier. If I were not so shy, I could talk about them all day. For example; a piece of netting with a rock in it and a rope threaded through the top meshes is a good anchor for your canoe or boat. With the rock tossed out your anchor kit weighs next to nothing. Of course, you may have difficulty finding another rock. Why burn your hands when boiling the kettle? Summer or winter brings the same danger, and a burn or cut can ruin a nice weekend or other outing. I always carry a good quality pair of oven mitts in my pack. It prevents burning my hands, or good winter mitts, and I can always wear them in a pinch.

Perhaps this is a good time to conclude, otherwise you will learn all my secret techniques.

THE SALTY FISH

Someone asked me one day what kind of fishing I liked best. For me the answer was simple: "Whatever kind I'm doing at the moment." Not a very satisfactory answer; depending on who asked the question. As I've grown older and realized you don't always have to prove something, the fishing has become more important than the fish. There must always be a purpose, or we would never attempt to do anything. However, the end result should never be allowed to take away the pleasure of pursuing it; even if the purpose is never achieved. For example, if you want to go for a walk, 'where' is important or you'd never start; 'how far' does not really matter.

Flowers River, Labrador, 1970

Sport Fishing

When sport fishing is mentioned, most people think of salmon and trout in the rivers and lakes. Until about thirty years ago I used to be the same. Now I think of catching rock cod near Chesley Flowers' fishing place in Flowers Bay, Labrador; sculpins off the wharf in Davis Inlet (the dogs like them — sand and all); cod off almost anywhere in the Province; mackerel off Woody Point; smelts in Terrigton Basin, Goose Bay; pike in the ponds along the 'Freedom Road' from Goose Bay to Churchill Falls and Esker; huge speckled trout in No Name and Park Lakes; caplin in Middle Cove; lake trout anywhere in Western Labrador; squid almost anywhere along the coast; mussels in Magic Arm, Bonavista Bay; mud trout in Lockyer's Waters; salmon in Biscay Bay, the Humber, Flowers, Hunt, Salmonier and a host of other rivers; and the noble char along the Labrador coast. All of them my favourite fish. Now if you pressed me I might be a little biased, one way or the other. I don't consider any kind of fishing beneath me because it gets me outdoors and, after all, we can still eat even if I don't catch any.

Salt Water base camp — Big Bay, 1989

Salt Water Fishing

With all due respect to inland fishing, there is a lot of healthy fun and satisfaction to be derived from fishing in the salt water. The sea is the mother of all life; the great provider, awesome and destructive but at the same time beautiful and bountiful. To and from it go salmon, char, trout, eel, smelt, gaspereau and a host of other species from their summer or winter places in the lakes and rivers. Its resident population, in unbelievable variety, ranges the world's seas and oceans.

The Noble Char

Charity begins at home, so they say, but not many in Newfoundland have received the kind of 'char'ity I mean. They can be caught in Western Brook, near St. Anthony, and perhaps other places along the Great Northern Peninsula. The prime fishing places for char are in Labrador and the Northwest Territories.

For me, the best char fishing is in the salt water when they are running in July and August, on their way back to the lakes and rivers to spawn. You can catch them with lures in the coves and along the beaches leading up the bays to the rivers.

Adlatok River, Labrador, 1980

Ujulok Falls, Labrador

North of Hamilton Inlet in Labrador is the prime area. Fishing is excellent in Ujutok Bay, off the big island in Big Bay, off the bars in Adlatok Bay, along the beach and off the wharf in Davis Inlet, in the coves in Nain Bay and all the way north to Nutak, Hebron, Saglek, Ramah, Ryan's Bay and beyond. Char Lake, between Hopedale and Davis Inlet is a favourite inland spot, as are Sangu Brook and Umiakovik Lake.

We like Flowers Bay, and to a lesser extent, Sangu Bay; both near Davis Inlet. In fact, though not having had the benefit of travelling the whole world, my favourite area in my known world is Davis Inlet. This encompasses Sangu Bay, Big Bay and Flowers Bay. This area is well forested by northern standards and has several beautiful rivers and lakes. In it you can conduct almost any type of outdoor activity as the seasons roll around.

Narrow, shallow runs or 'tickles' between islands, or the constrictions of bays, where the flowing and ebbing tides resemble rapids, are called 'rattles' in Labrador. Though not exploited, most of them are excellent places for salt water

Our camp at Sangu Bay, 1969

fishing. You can stand on the shore to do it. If you wade you must remember it is not a river, and it is easy to be cut off by the rising tides. Red devil lures, and spinners, guarantee fish. For the purist, there is tremendous fishing with streamer flies and buck bugs using a conventional fly rod.

Flowers Bay, just southeast of Davis Inlet, is really three bays; outer, middle and inner, with a narrow entrance to the latter two. The Flowers, a noble salmon and char river, flows into the inner bay, while several small brooks flow into the others. They are also the habitat of numerous speckled trout. These trout come out to feed in the 'Rattles' between the middle and outer bays. Every salmon and char must travel through them on their way into the Flowers, and other brooks; what a glorious place!

On the left shore of the first 'Rattle' is a flat grassy stretch of beach, covered with driftwood and backed by a steep cliff. A spring flows out of that cliff cold enough to make your father shiver when you drink the water. On the right are rocky shallows which curve around to where the old Flowers' homestead used to be; the original white settlers in the Bay.

Planking a salmon, Flowers River, Labrador, 1969
"Larry is surprised"

On one trip, we set up our camp on the grassy flat, near the spring; Dave and Doris Butler, of the Hudson's Bay Company, Shirley and myself. We had two sleeping tents, suitably spaced for privacy. We also had a large cook tent, with a trapper's stove, positioned so that we could watch the sunsets, and look up and down the bay. We kept a large canning pot on the stove. You could boil an egg, wash the dishes or have a bath; what comfort! When the wind changed, the stove used to blow smoke rings out the draft hole to add to the hilarity. The fishing was so good that we had to take turns catching supper. We had to walk about ten feet back of the cook tent to catch those speckled trout and char; what hardship!

Have you ever caught a char in the salt water? They are beautiful fish, strong as a salmon. Though of the trout family they are shaped like salmon, but the lines are better; more delicate. They are greenish colour on the back, whitish on the belly, with what appears to be a 'rubbing strip' on the sides. In the fresh water they change colour, becoming darker on the back and orange along the belly.

When you hook a salmon it can go up, down or across the pool. Some have been known to go farther, or even bore down to the bottom of the pool and stubbornly stay there. But a char hooked in the salt water has much more scope; there is nothing between you and it, and Ireland. They range between three and thirty pounds; what a fight! What a pleasure to look at or to eat!

Those skilful women outdid Dave and me. We had a lot of laughs, noble feeds and fantastic views. Now and then we talked sensibly and seriously. It all helped us realize who we really were.

I often think of the many times I've seen the geese and ducks fly along the cliff, up or down the 'Rattle' to the ponds or flats in Flowers or Big Bay; the big speckles chasing a streamer; the warm tent and the delicate sky as the sun eased down; and that spring water compared to what we drink in the cities.

What a paradise the Flowers family had! What a pity life at the time did not provide the leisure that we now enjoy! It is possible, however, that their appreciation of what they had exceeded ours.

THE NORTHEAST

Perhaps you have heard of Roddickton. Roddickton is at the head of Canada Bay, set on the fringe of the Long Range Mountains, which run roughly south to north for 600 miles in western Newfoundland; the entire length of the Great Northern Peninsula. Wherever you stand in Roddickton there is an ever changing vista of sea and mountains, varied by sun, mist and wind. You leave the Trans-Canada Highway at Deer Lake and drive through Gros Morne National Park up the peninsula to Plum Point. From there you drive east across the peninsula to Roddickton; a trip to soothe the soul!

Into Canada Bay flow several rivers, one of which is the Northeast. All have their merits but I like the Northeast best. It flows under the highway bridge a few miles from Roddickton where it's clean, clear water meets the Bay. On a bright day you can see not only to the bottom from above, but through the pools from the side, and watch the silver flash of salmon as they move suddenly for some reason known only to themselves.

Feeder Lake, near Portland Creek — Zinck and Goodyear

Drink the water in your cupped hands, fill your kettle, wash, or clean your teeth. How many places do you know where that can still be done? Ask yourself, "How long will it last if we continue to be careless?"

There are eight good salmon pools on the Northeast. Three of them are a short distance from the highway. Of the five inside pools the farthest is five miles, and consequently it is designated 'Five Mile.' Many years ago there was a logging operation in that area and the Northeast was one of the many rivers used to float logs to the holding booms in the Bay. That meant a series of primitive dams at the run-out of large steadies in the river. Logging has ceased but the remnants of some of the old dams help form good pools, above and below them. Five Mile has the wreck of two old dams and provides three separate places to fish.

You can reach these pools by walking the river. However, most fishermen prefer to follow the old logging road, with branch paths to the pools. The road is muddy and rough, requiring hip-waders. The mosquitoes and black flies are friendly; they come around you all the time, biting occasionally so that you'll notice.

I remember the first time I fished at Four Mile. Ray Zinck and I walked in early one morning and sized up the pool. We crossed a clear, cold spring flowing over marble chips, and which cut into the slow-moving water of the steady. A salmon jumped in a most unlikely place so Ray sent out a 'Green Islander.' On the fourth cast his reel began to sing. With whatever patience I could muster, I waited until he beached the salmon. Not big, about six pounds, but bright as silver.

Moving upstream, I looked through the clear water. There were six or seven salmon moving up through the swift water and they stopped in a shallow pool. In no time I flicked a small black moose hair-silvertip towards them. A salmon rose as the 'hitched' fly swam across the current. Even an experienced fisherman finds it difficult to wait, but a salmon rising to a hitched fly always takes it on the way down. A quick pluck determined it had taken. After giving a couple more to set the hook, I got the rod up as high as I could. One, two, three jumps with alternate singing and clacking reel and the fish was on a tight line in the slack water. After considerable resistance, I put its nose on the beach and grabbed it by the small of the tail.

That morning we caught our limit before we took our packs off. It was 9:00 o'clock, so we had our lunch anyway; there by the marble spring, flowing into that fabulous pool.

On this particular trip I was by myself. Zinck and I had planned a six week canoeing and fishing trip to Northern Labrador. However, illness in the family, and an unbelievable flow of arctic ice disrupting shipping, forced us to cancel. It's not that the Northeast is second best; just a good alternative!

There are good accommodations at Roddickton, but when I'm by myself I live simply and sleep in the back of the truck. That sounds rougher than reality. The truck has a watertight fibreglass cap, carpeted box and a four inch foam mattress. Overhead hangs a mosquito bar,* giving full protection from the flies and good ventilation. With the back window up, I can lie in bed and count the stars or listen in comfort to the rain on the roof. With a canvas canopy over the back there is adequate protection from the rain. A van tent provides additional protection, and serves as a livingroom. It is really amazing that you can leave all that, fully equipped and unattended by the side of the road for days on end, and not have to worry about theft. Yes, there are honest people in the world!

It was the 10th of July, 1991, and there were few salmon in the river. Before leaving home I phoned Roddickton and learned that, because of so much drift ice, the salmon run was late. When I drove out to Roddickton and Englee, I saw what

---

* Fine mosquito netting draped over the bunk to bar the pests from your sleeping quarters, without hampering the flow of fresh air.

my friend meant. There were large icebergs and drift ice everywhere.

The first salmon of the year is always crucial. No matter how many fish you've caught over the years, there is always a nagging doubt about your ability to do it again. Perhaps it's something like sex, when you're getting old.

I got up at 5:00 a.m., had a good breakfast with two mugs of coffee, and walked directly to Five Mile. About four miles in the old road, thinking about salmon, I came face to face with a big cow moose. It rarely happens in hunting season. We were both startled momentarily, but in two strides she was gone. A friend once told me that every moose carries its own tree to hide behind.

There was a lone fisherman at Five Mile when I got there. Judging by where he was fishing, I thought he wasn't too familiar with the pools. While jointing up my rod I watched him casting below the old dam. There is the remains of an older dam about a hundred feet upstream, and this forms a narrow, fast pool. I walked out to the flat rock on the far side. This rock has some sort of algae growing on it which looks like a smear of red paint. I've seen the same thing on the Upper Humber River.

Starting there, I cast across the head of the pool and slowly worked the fly down to where the salmon usually lay. It was dull and overcast, the effect of the drift ice, and the green islander fly with the junglecock eyes combed across the pool. After about five to ten minutes, a fish rose in the usual place. Pure reflex pulled the fly away. That is one of the most common reasons for not hooking a salmon. I hauled in the line, keeping my finger on the spot which would indicate the length, and waited for a while.

The salmon took the fly on the third cast, jumped twice, and was gone.

Having seen what happened, the other fellow came up and we talked for a while. He confirmed that this was his first visit to Five Mile. Since he seemed to be a decent chap I showed him where to fish, but nothing rose after. We then waded out and looked into the pool; it was barren. That little place is a passing pool, where the salmon rest before moving into the big steady. I learned never to look into the pool first since it's so narrow and shallow that the salmon move away when they see you.

On the way back I worked all the pools without seeing a sign of a fish, and arrived back at the camp footsore and dog tired. A refreshing drink gave me enough energy to cook supper, and then I went to bed; didn't count many stars.

Five a.m. came earlier than I wanted and it was raining when I got up. The roof of that so-called super van tent leaked enough to make a pool of water on the floor. There was also water in the frying pan, but that didn't affect my appetite. Soon I was on my way, shrouded in a rain parka. There were fresh moose tracks everywhere.

Shortly after I arrived at Five Mile, three guys came down from Cook's Steady in a power boat and hogged the pool. After a while I walked back to Four Mile. There was nothing there except two moose feeding along shore. It was obvious the main salmon run hadn't started. Next, I walked down to the Falls. Now it's not much of a falls, compared to other rivers but there are two small pools, one above and one below. They would each be about fifty feet in length, with very fast water. On the far side of the upper pool there is a submerged reef. Usually salmon come up the chute over the falls and lie for a short time inside that reef.

As you come down the barely discernible path along the cliff, you break out of the alders at the foot of a rock pool formed when the river is in flood. You have to get through this to approach the upper salmon pool; the bottom is treacherously slippery.

To get to the standing spot it is necessary to wade along a submerged ledge, and then over a tangle of rocks to a flat rock about a foot under water. A right handed person can cast with some comfort. However, I'm left handed, and it's tricky when you strip out enough line to reach the salmon. There is an unfriendly tree to the back of you, angled out from the cliff, which must have the finest collection of salmon flies in Newfoundland; some of mine are amongst them. It's a beautiful spot, nevertheless, secluded from the trail, and not fished much because of its trickery.

My blue charm swam across the pool repeatedly. After several casts it swept about half way to where the salmon usually lie. Suddenly, I hooked a fish in the chute just above the top of the falls. When it jumped, I saw it was a very small grilse. The problem at this pool is trying to prevent the fish from going over the falls. So, it's up rod and work your way to shore, along the ledge and into the slackest water, in a little crevice. Having managed to do that, I released the little salmon; it was about two pounds and covered with sea lice. Never before have I caught one that small, fresh in from the sea. It must have been mature, because they don't usually return except to participate in the spawning process. There must be many exceptions to conventional wisdom about salmon.

The situation looked hopeful, so I sat down and had a snack while waiting for the pool to settle. Back at the standing place, I began the casting process. When the blue charm finally reached the reef, and combed across, up came a fish. Waiting a while, I cast at the same spot. However, the wind must have been in cahoots with that fly-catching tree because, try as I did, I lost the leader and all.

Once all was ready again, up came the salmon. After a suitable interval the hook was set, and the battle began. The fish jumped four times, twice while I was working my way ashore. With the rod up all the time, the salmon came almost into that little crevice three or four times; finally I had it by the tail. It was salmon number one; about six pounds and at the legal length. When it was cleaned, and the offal put up for roaming mink, I had another snack. This was great; no competition and the world's most pleasant surroundings.

About half an hour later I repeated the process and landed another fish. The daily limit was two. However, as I took the fly out, that salmon gave a hefty flick. My grip slackened and down it went into the flood pool. I think I did every ballet step known before cornering it in a shallow place in the pool. It is wise to have a 'killing stick' near you at all times.

It was a pleasant feeling, walking out with two salmon in the pack. On stopping at One Mile, there were three people fishing in the wrong places. I showed them where to stand. Later, when I was cooking supper, one of them came by and offered to put my fish in his freezer in Roddickton; courtesy pays off?

The next day was unproductive, perhaps because of the ice and the wrong tides. That discouraged the fishermen and now I had the river to myself again. There is a degree of selfishness in all of us, and I got up at 4:00 o'clock the next morning. Being a dog for punishment, I worked all the pools in as far as Five Mile without success. When I began to work my way back I stopped at Four Mile for lunch, and sat there listening to a bird I've heard only there. Its call sounded clearly like "Jigger, jigger, jigger Jim." My name is not Jim. While contemplating the pool and surroundings, a salmon jumped well out. After wading out as far as I could, I was at the limit of my casting ability when it took the fly. It was much easier to land that fish there than at the Falls. Much heartened, I got a second salmon about 3:00 p.m.

I won't bore you with further details, but when the week was over I had ten salmon; the season limit. That was at a time when the run was late due to ice conditions. That indicates what the Northeast is like in a normal year.

As I drove down the peninsula towards Gros Morne and Deer Lake, with the sparkling sea on the right and the spectacular mountains on the left, I felt a sense of well-being that only such experiences can bring. Perhaps it's your turn next!

WHEN I WAS A RANGER

WAITING OUT A BLIZZARD

You know what happens around St. John's, or any city, when there is a bad winter forecast. Sometimes everything grinds to a halt before the snow comes. Of course, business and government rarely announce closures because they will be stuck with paying full salaries. It's amazing how many are glad to stay home, especially if they have unused sick leave.

Who can blame them, with their comfortable homes, television, tape decks, video games, VCRs, numerous hobbies, books and a few unfinished jobs around the house. Why, the only thinking a person has to do is about what type of entertainment to choose.

It wasn't always like that. Where I grew up we were lucky. It was a company town and the electricity didn't go off as frequently as now. Those with radios could be assured of a continuing level of static interspersed with a bit of news, courtesy of Gerald S. Doyle, and all the Wilf Carter we could stand. We couldn't afford a radio but didn't feel a bit deprived since the only radio on the street belonged to our next door neighbour. They wanted us to share the programs and set their radio up on their pantry windowsill where we got maximum benefit for free.

Some years ago when I was a Newfoundland Ranger in a certain place we got talking about radios. This friend told me about the first radio they ever had in their community. Apparently the local merchant, called Sam, bought the first radio. Now he had two brothers, Job and Gus. Job lived near Sam's store, while Gus lived up on the hill some distance away. Everybody was really intrigued by the radio and Sam's store filled up every day that first winter. Mostly the programs were static. One day Job came into the store and said, as he always did;

"Anything on the radio today Sam?"

"Yes boy", Sam Said, "Lots of static, but I got the forecast too."

"Good," Job said, "What's the forecast?"

"Well Job, boy, it's bad. I allows Gus will be blowed off the hill."

"Why is that Sam?"

"Well, Job, boy, they said in the forecast the wind in to Gus's is going to be up to eighty miles an hour."

You may think I'm rambling. If that's a sin, a lot of people will have to do penance. The point is that when I was a Ranger in Nain, the entertainment was even more skimpy than when I was a child. That first winter I didn't have a radio, and very few books. I read the labels on all of the cans of my winter rations. Had the labels been bilingual I would have got a head start on French. That's when you find out if you have inner resources. More importantly, you learn to appreciate the inner strengths of other people.

What could you do in the north in 1946, or any year when you are isolated from people and gadgets, when the snow is thick and swirling and the wind shaking whatever shelter you are in. When it's zero-zero there are no streets, no lights and none of those vibrating, comforting sounds that drift back from the snowplough or the late plane.

Well, you can sleep; but how much? Write letters in January for the June mail boat? How meaningful to you, the writer. Eat? There's a limit to that, especially if you are on the trail and the grub has to last. Of course you can always talk; but the topics are limited and not always by your very sparse knowledge of the language.

You can always think, but the harder you try the more frustrating it becomes. It takes years to learn that the most productive thinking takes place without trying. Of course, there has to be something inside the skull before it can swirl around and come out in some other form.

Mostly you find yourself playing the universal game; cards, especially 45s and 120s. How common and dull, you say; what, no bridge?

Cards bridge the gap between all classes and cultures, and they sure pass the time. All of a sudden it's time for damper-dogs* and tea, before you unroll your sleeping bag.

But cards were sinful in those days. The Moravian Missionaries forbade all card playing. Tiddlywinks and Finch were alright of course, but cards! Why, it was the Devil's game; the first step into sin. By agreement the Hudson's Bay Company, and later the government store, wouldn't stock them. I never learned to play cards until I went into Moravian territory. We never had a pack of cards in our house. The Inuit, taught me.

You may ask where they got the cards. There were several sources. The odd pack was purchased from those sinful Newfoundlanders on the fishing schooners at the Queen's Lakes and September Harbour, to mention two places. A few worn out packs were salvaged by the maid at the store manager's house; but mainly they were bootleg — they made them.

Most of you are not old enough to remember the brand of tea we had during the War. China, Ceylon and India must have sold millions of pounds in the early part of the War. Every patriotic merchant sold 'Victory' tea, mostly in half pound packages.

There were cardboard squares with neatly rounded corners in the ends of those packages. With a pencil they made nice cards for those with good eyesight. That was in the days before ballpoint pens and the few with ink pens couldn't use them because the ink was invariably frozen. Many an argument arose as to what particular card it was and some people

---

* Bread dough, cooked on the top of the stove.

must be bad friends to this day. I've never taken cards seriously since.

One time we came across the Kiglapiat Mountains from Nutak by dogteam on the way to Nain. We became stormbound in what used to be Port Manvers, just under the southern side of the mountains. It was a rough trip and the dog-team driver and I were sure glad to get there. There were only two families at that place. Conversation was exhausted more quickly than usual, and out came the cards. By now they knew I wasn't a spy for the missionary.

I tell you, it was quite a sight; fifty two Victory tea package ends. Can't remember exactly how high the deck was, but we had to deal them in five or six lots. I was never the most dexterous, even with plastic cards. The darned things wouldn't slip either, but that didn't bother our host. The open flour sack was nearby and you would never believe what a dusting of flour did for the dealer; you could shuffle those five or six lots in no time. We had a barrel (or is it a bag) of fun and the storm was almost over before we knew it. "Go ahead policekuluk, your deal."

LIKE IT OR LUMP IT

Ex-Newfoundland Rangers, like lots of older people, often talk about the old days; reluctantly, of course. Generally speaking, isolation in Newfoundland and Labrador dictated that most people operated within a fairly small area. While their experiences were often interesting and hazardous, and sometimes downright terrible, they didn't have the opportunity to see our country and its conditions as did the Rangers. Please note the term 'country!' I remember picking up a mental patient in a certain village. During the long escort to St. John's, in one of his more lucid moments, he told me he had never before been out of sight of the place where he was born; except when the fog came in. He was forty-two years old. Of course Newfoundland sea-dogs were a notable exception to the rule.

It is hard to believe what it was like a few short years ago. I often see that unbelieving glint in the listener's eye when past experiences are being told. Even my own kids had to hear it from others before they really believed what the 'old man' told them. Dramatic change is not confined to this province alone.

Conditions were different in many respects. The biggest liars are those who go around trying to prove they never had it as bad as people like me. I know people who have spent the past thirty years trying to prove they were never poor. The unfortunate thing is that, relative to the lifestyles of their listeners, their tales are more easily swallowed. I think it's more important to remember, and acknowledge, your background. It is probably more important to do it with the luxury of distance, and change, largely created by your own efforts.

Perhaps it really doesn't matter if people believe your

accounts of the past or not. Maybe it's the telling that counts, and whether they enjoy them. If some interest in the past is aroused, that's a bonus. I happen to believe that the greatest benefit flows to the storyteller who is able to strip away the outer layer of what he or she now is and expose the frailties, irrational streaks and toughness, which, by daily recognition within, created that outer layer.

Isolation certainly has physical boundaries, but the real boundaries are those which we allow our minds to create. All that is modified by where we fit in relation to others — so living in Nain in the late 1940s differed from St. Anthony only in relation to population, availability of local services and external contacts like mail and the wireless telegraph. Perhaps I could admit to a few other differences if you force me.

The last boat for the year, the M.V. *Winifred Lee*, used to meet the S.S. *Kyle* at Hopedale around the last of September. It then made its trip north to Davis Inlet, Nain, Nutak and Hebron. It made the return trip, arriving at Nain around the middle of October, and then went south to St. John's. The yearly rations for the single Ranger usually arrived on that trip and were put off on the way north. A full year's supply of food and household items; adequate, but not sumptuous.

Mary Sillett, Nain, 1946

There was even two bottles of medicinal brandy; sickness always struck the Detachment with unbelievable swiftness.

Government purchasing procedures haven't changed much over the years: only transportation. The eggs used to be bought in the spring for fall delivery. Since they were Canadian 'case eggs' God knows when they were last seen by the hens which laid them. Potatoes, onions, carrots and turnips were either frozen on arrival, or quickly thereafter. It took me two years to learn from old Mrs. Ford, that as long as you kept them frozen, they were usable.

The last night the boat spent at Nain on the way south there was always a party. I strongly suspect that some of my rations went back aboard the *Winifred Lee*. Anyway, it was all fun because we wouldn't see them or anyone else from 'outside' until around the end of June. Did you ever get your Christmas parcels in June or July?

The Ranger Force Detachment was perhaps the best building in Nain, with the exception of the Moravian Mission and Post Manager's houses. It was twenty by twenty feet, with a front and back porch. These porches measured two by two. The building had clapboard on the posts, and ten-test wallboard inside. What about insulation? Well, that came annually when the snow drifted up around the house. Automatic

Ranger Force detachment building, Nain, 1946

insulation arrived just when you thought you'd freeze to death. We got all those luxuries for the noble salary of $45.00 a month.

I suppose it is wrong to impute ulterior motives to Headquarters; but that building became so uncomfortable that I was forced to go on dogteam patrol to keep warm and preserve my sanity. While away the cans of food froze solid: go — freeze; return — thaw; maybe. Walking across the flimsy floor used to cause those rounded cans to rock back and forth. That reminded me I couldn't afford to throw them out. I ate the stuff anyway: so much for 'dated' foods!

"What has all this to do with lumps?" you ask. Ah, sugar; how sweet it is! Newfoundlanders were once noted for their honesty; but until Sgt. Delaney started shipping those sacks of sugar on the S.S. *Kyle* in tongue-and-groove boxes, the sugar was always missing when the rations were checked off.

That first winter there was a surplus of sugar on hand, so the box wasn't broken open until sometime in January. There it was; a solid one hundred pound lump. It weighed almost as much as I did after several months of my own nourishing cooking.

After beating off a piece with the ax, I tried grating it with the cheese grater. At any rate, that's what we called it because it was years later that I learned of coleslaw. It 'grated' on my nerves so much that I beat it into three or four large lumps. Whenever I had tea or coffee, I just soaked off a corner and put that big lump on a towel on the table. It looked like something Nain dogs used before they discovered fire hydrants. The only eyebrows, or legs, raised was by the Missionaries; they didn't have to live like me.

How irrational, you think. Well, it was a while before I would admit to anything but the 'ration!' But what is the difference? Who did I have to impress all the way up there, and why engage in all that useless labour? The best hotels and inns still allow me into their dining rooms; like it or lump it?

THE BEARSKIN KOULITAK

What a change there has been in clothing over the years. We have gone from animal skins to man-made skins like wool, cotton, nylon and a host of other fabrics. Styles have changed considerably as well. Outdoor clothing has improved a considerable amount in comfort, durability and appearance. Sometimes I wonder though about the utility of skimpy hoods, bulky collars and flap-less pockets which drift full of snow. These and other serious design flaws mar even the most expensive parkas, jackets and vests. However, it is difficult to beat the design, materials and workmanship of skilled Indian and Inuit people. They utilized the things available to them. It seemed obvious that if skins served animals well, they would also serve people.

The best sewing thread at that time was 'sinew,' the large back muscles of the caribou. When dried and shredded, these sinews became very strong thread. Sealskin boots with carefully lapped seams were made completely waterproof as the wet sinew swelled and filled the needle holes. Of course, that applied only to the untanned skins. I have a full sinew in my collection of native materials. It is now almost a novelty as the art of cutting out and preparing them is nearly lost. In fact, the craft shop in Nain sells factory made 'sinews.'

The fur ruff around the hood of the parka or koulitak (ku-li-tak) was made of wolverine, wolf or dog. They are relatively frost-free, in that order. Most people are surprised to learn that dogs are fur bearing animals. I suspect that many a tourist has gone home with a wolf pelt which was once a dog. A friend of ours once had a Labrador retriever which was much admired by a certain old lady. Whenever she saw the

107

Cyril J. Goodyear
#158 Newfoundland Ranger Force
Nain, Labrador, 1946

dog she used to remark, "My wouldn't he make a lovely pair of mitts."

Seal and caribou were preferred for koulitaks; parkas to you. However, occasionally other skins were used and many people were not knowledgeable enough to understand their relative merits; I was one of them.

Shortly after WWII, I was discharged from the Royal Canadian Air Force and joined the Newfoundland Ranger Force. For the benefit of those born since 1949 the Rangers were our national police force, patterned after the RCMP, and absorbed into the Force after Newfoundland joined Canada. In any event, I was transferred to Nain in late August. One of the first things we used to do was familiarize ourselves with our district and get to know as many people as possible. That policy appears to have gone out of style these days, we don't know the police and they don't know us; not even the crooks. Not long after I arrived in Nain I took a walk across the hills to a place called Kauk. It got its name because the headland which distinguishes the harbour entrance is shaped like a human forehead. A comfortable five mile walk takes you there. Richard White lived there and operated a trading post. He was a very sharp trader and one of the most interesting people I ever met, though I must admit he didn't need to exhaust his skills on me.

I was amazed at the variety of things at his trading post.

He persuasively assisted me in looking things over. One item in particular caught my fancy; it was a bearskin koulitak. The skins were glossy and well matched and, of course, it was a real bargain at $25.00.

After some hesitation, since I only earned $45.00 a month, I was finally persuaded to buy on the basis that winter was coming. Other factors entered in; the total northern clothing issue to Rangers was two pairs of sealskin boots a year. We had to buy our own parkas. Having tried it on several times, and after several cups of tea with Mr. White, he put the koulitak in a sugar sack and I walked proudly back to Nain. I was now equipped for the long arctic winter, and could hardly wait for it to come.

The days dragged on by with only a few snow flurries for encouragement. I waited for about a month, admiring the koulitak every time I passed the peg on which it hung. Finally, some snow came but not sufficient to justify wearing my koulitak. I don't suppose there was a full length mirror in Nain, unless the Moravian missionary's wife owned one. Perhaps they were scarce all over Newfoundland and Labrador in those days. In any event, I didn't have the benefit of viewing myself in full in those beautiful bearskins.

As the days passed I became more and more anxious to wear the koulitak, but all I could do was put in on and look at myself in the small wall mirror. You know those small six by eight mirrors with the white enamelled frame? The darned thing was not wide enough to show my face with the hood up.

However, I got a reasonable view and fancied myself just like Peary at the North Pole or Amundsen at the South. It gave me some comfort to look at what little I could see of myself because the thickness of the fur made me as big as a bear, so to speak. Of course, I kept a weather eye out for visitors as I would have felt rather silly if anyone had seen me wearing the thing around the house.

Finally we had a big snowstorm and I waited anxiously for enough to pile up so that it would fully justify wearing fur clothing. On a beautiful morning after the storm, I donned my koulitak and walked out the front door. The world was white and gleaming and frost nipped at my moist nostrils as I surveyed the harbour and the big cliff beyond. How my koulitak stood out against the pure white snow.

As I walked through the snow towards the Mission House, I noticed several husky dogs perking up with interest. Now those were the days before the skidoo was invented and everybody had dogs. In fact there were about 500 dogs in Nain, nearly all running loose.

More and more dogs showed interest in my fur apparel. I became very uneasy, walking warily and slowly and looking all around. Suddenly two dogs made for me and I turned and ran. A large number of other dogs joined in the chase. I 'bearly' made it back to the house, thoroughly frightened.

Needless to say, I never wore that magnificent koulitak again. It is still somewhat comforting to me that it made several cosy scatter-rugs for that cold floor.

POLICE BRUTALITY

You have all heard of police brutality? Probably you've heard it from a succession of someone's? Of course you have never experienced it yourselves and therefore never had occasion to complain about it. I'm told that the Charter of Rights and Freedoms has changed all that and there is no longer any need to fear the police; only the crooks. People have to be in constant fear of them now but before Newfoundland joined Canada, the police were feared. Perhaps that is why we had so few criminals.

Anyway, I know what it was like because I was once a policeman; or should that be a police person? Before Confederation few places had running water except when the buckets leaked. Lawns were designed for sheep, goats and those cute little Newfie ponies. There were no rubber hoses, so we couldn't use them, and the only rehabilitative brutality was a whack on the jaw for adult crooks, and a kick in the rear for juveniles. Rehabilitation didn't cost anything either, only a few band aids and liniment. These days it takes an army of criminologists and social workers to convince the crooks they didn't do anything wrong.

There were very few jails in those days, so we were brutal enough to let everybody but the murderers go home until they were tried and sentenced. That way they slept in their own beds and ate their own food. The Mainlanders found out about this and they now believe they invented it. When a person became a prisoner in the old days, a policeman's wife fed the prisoner better than her husband; what hardship! Of course, travelling to the Penitentiary in St. John's was no fun. The trains all ran in the wee hours of the morning so that they would arrive in or depart the city at the convenience of the

Townies. The second class seats were made of wood. Those slat-like marks are a topic of conversation every time I have a medical. However, the food on the train was excellent and hasn't been equalled since, between here and Vancouver. We heard that Donald Gordon, former President of the Canadian National Railways got the job because he reduced the size of the plates so that the meals would appear bigger.

What has all this got to do with Nunatsuak? Well, that kind of activity takes place in 'the big land' too. If you keep reading, relevance will surface.

Once upon a time in a certain little place in Newfoundland some bad people committed certain offenses. I put on my sleuthing cap and was fortunate to catch them. Behold, one day the Magistrate came on one of his infrequent visits and, on hearing the evidence, convicted them. Except for one, fines were imposed. That unfortunate individual was sentenced to a term in Her Majesty's Penitentiary as a guest of the taxpayers.

Court was over by noon but the train wasn't due until the early hours of the morning, assuming it was on time. There were no roads or other means of transport, and no local jail. So the prisoner and I became prisoners of each other. If you have never been a brutal policeman you can never know the nagging fear that your prisoner, usually bigger than you, will escape. That would mean you would have to look for another job. Without a safe little cell, his brothers might even assist him. There were no reinforcements to call up, even if you had a telephone.

So I took him to the local boarding house and fed him well. People are more passive with a bellyful. The afternoon dragged, with not too much animated conversation. Finally suppertime rolled around and we ate another huge meal. How I wish I could eat like that now.

The people who owned the boarding house were friends of mine, as you will see. So they said, "Goodyear, you got a

Goodyear in winter garb, 1950s

long night ahead of you." You see, you don't sleep when you have a prisoner in those circumstances; but how you want to!

It was prime salmon time and someone suggested I go fishing. Perhaps you think this was unusual? Of course, but it would take the prisoner's mind off his sorry plight and I would put up with any tedium and hardship to achieve that. I borrowed a rod, flies and a landing net, and, with the prisoner's complete agreement, we went up to the 'Guzzle Hole.' You may know where it is, but further explanation is unnecessary; perhaps unwise.

Many people have fished the Guzzle Hole without success. It is a beautiful spot with high cliffs on both sides opening out into a picturesque pool. At the narrowest point, at the head of the pool, there are two partly submerged rocks and fishermen usually stand on them and fish down into the pool. That's where they make their mistake, because the salmon lie nose-up to one of those rocks. You have to use a short line and drop the fly on the right spot. It is important to stand back so the fish can't see you.

The prisoner was not a fisherman so I gave him instructions in case I hooked a fish. After dropping the fly a couple of times I rose a fish, promptly forgetting the prisoner. On pausing a short time, I flicked out my fly and hooked it. The prisoner started to shout with excitement, reminding me he was there.

Now the fun began. With the fish on, taking the odd jump, I had to go around the cliff and pass the rod around two snaggy trees in order to bring it to a level landing place. There was the prisoner with the landing net, issuing all kinds of instructions. When I brought the salmon in, after two tries, he scooped it into the net. That prisoner was as proud as any professional guide.

We sat down on a rock and had a smoke; two good buddies. He insisted I catch some more and with great reluctance, bearing in mind my heavy responsibilities, I walked up over the cliff and cast out again.

That was in the days when you could catch four or more salmon. I've forgotten the exact number. There is no necessity of boring you with the details, but we hooked and landed three more salmon. My companion was glad he was a prisoner because that was the first time he ever engaged in such a sport.

Just about 'duckish'* we went back to the boarding house. We had a great big lunch and a grand chat. It seemed like no time at all before the train arrived and we sat down on those hard seats, having practised on the rocks at the Guzzle Hole. The prisoner slept all the way to St. John's, while I focused one eye on him from time to time to make sure he was still with me. We had a scrumptious breakfast in the dining car before leaving the train and parting company. He never got into trouble again.

I suppose if I recommended that type of rehabilitative activity for prisoners and parolees, somebody would say, "There's a catch to it."

---

* Twilight, when it's still light enough to see, but too dark to begin anything useful.

LITERACY

In one of my other lives, since I've had several official ones, I used to operate a police boat around Bonavista Bay. It was said that I knew every rock in the Bay, because I struck them all. It just goes to show how little the Canadians knew about us. The Royal Canadian Mounted Police, that national symbol, was just as uninformed when they took over the Newfoundland Ranger Force. They assumed all Newfoundlanders were seamen.

RCMP, Glovertown, 1954

Functional

There were few roads in those days, especially around Bonavista Bay; hence the boat! A patrol took about ten days, and the weather factor was more important than it is now. Fortunately ignorance overcame timidity and we cruised around the Bay with reasonable efficiency. Investigations took us to those fantastic and prosperous islands, and other settlements, which the 'resettlement program' has since destroyed.

The police boat was thirty-six feet long and safety required a second person aboard. We used to hire local people as deckhands. They were all personable and the trips, though sometimes hazardous for various reasons, were mostly enjoyable. It was a pleasant and valuable experience; floating through local history.

One of my sailing companions was a most 'able' seaman. He had a good sense of humour, a prerequisite for the job, and was game for anything. However, he couldn't read or write. This small deficiency only became known when the time came for him to sign a receipt for his wages. It bothered me that such a powerhouse of energy, knowledge and ability was constantly embarrassed. I agonized over this problem for some time. Finally, on one trip out the Bay, I gave him a large pad of foolscap with his name signed at the top. I told him that if he couldn't sign his name at the end of the trip, he would not be hired again. There was no indication that he ever practised, but work took me away from the boat for hours.

When we returned, I delayed paying him for over a week. Finally I went down to his house and his wife told me he was out in the shed. We talked about everything except his pay. Finally, he said, "I have something to show you." He took a lumber crayon out of his pocket and signed his name on the side of a large cornflake carton. He was as proud as Punch, and his smile clearly reflected it.

An Apology

I used to talk about that with some pride; never mentioning his name. What a contribution to literacy! Fortunately, we have the ability to re-think, and now I am ashamed of what I did to that fine man. He is gone now, and whether or not he ever learned to read; I most humbly apologize to him through all you literate people.

"What?" you say, "There's no need to apologize for that!" But, my friends, just think about it. Society, through its literate people, has taught us to shame those who can't read or write, those who are below a certain school grade, those perceived to be in a lower occupation or who have no occupation at all; but can do a multitude of things. The highly literate should develop a guilt complex, until they come to respect people for what they do; not for what they say or write. Did you ever meet a university professor, or people of similar breed, who felt shame or was put down by society because the only thing they could do was talk or write?

Think of all the literate people who can't drive a nail, saw a board, build a boat or house, or even find their way through the woods. My friend had only one deficiency, in a whole range of skills. Those who looked down on him — including me — had many.

The Shame Factor

Criminologists, psychiatrists and their associates have removed the shame factor from crime; to the detriment of society. Why can't we have a 'degree' of common sense in the approach to literacy? Like many children during the Great Depression, I heard one theme all through school. "Now, Cyril, you better attend to your studies. You don't want to be a logger like your father do you?" Thank all gods I never became ashamed of my father, because I saw what he could do. The 'functionally illiterate' built this country; as they did all other countries. As one old fellow from Wesleyville used to say, "When you got 'nar bit of education, that's when you got to use your brains."

RUDOLPH WAS EMBARRASSED

Whenever old-timers gather there is some talk about the present, very little about the future, and much about the past. That's what stories are made of; the futuristic stuff appeals to a limited audience. It also teaches few lessons; only the past can do that, and only the distant past allows the storyteller to be honest in its telling. You see, if you look at things in the legal sense, the statute of limitations runs out on most things after a few years. If you think I'm going to make any serious admissions here; you're wrong, as there is no crime in being truthful.

It is common for old folks to remember the past, be critical of the present, and be afraid of the future. Those themes are as old as humanity itself. I recall reading Egyptian history, written some five thousand years ago, where the writer expressed dire concern for the then current generation. While that theme is expressed in every age, about every generation, it is not all hogwash. All old-timers are not without knowledge and experience. Sometimes their past careers outshine those of their critics.

Take police work for example; it is not hard to remember when everybody knew the police in their community, but look at the situation now. The only time a police-person speaks to you now is if you, or somebody you know, is in trouble. If you have occasion to complain to them about something, it has to fall into a clearly and narrowly defined category or they won't talk to you. Even more frustrating is the fact that after 4:30 to 5:00 p.m. their office doors are locked. There is never anybody in before 9:00 in the morning. If you are on the highway, with almost no traffic, and happen to push your foot down unconsciously, you will get a ticket. The same thing applies if snow slides down your car roof and obscures your rear window.

You see, at one time discretion was the order of the day; but that takes commonsense. It also takes some understanding that members of the public are not inferior to the police. There is a degree of arrogance involved in the conduct of some police; arrogance stifles intelligence. Perhaps one of the factors in bringing about that state of affairs is the narrowly based training, and the tunnel-vision that it generates.

Before confederation, the police had a multitude of duties. Added to these obligations were social welfare, fish and game law enforcement, customs and excise, inspection of logging camps, etc., which brought the police into contact

with people from all walks of life. They got to know everybody and earned their trust; that fact alone works wonders in solving crime.

Those of us who went into the Royal Canadian Mounted Police in 1950 took our people-knowledge, flexibility and discretion with us. We were of, and from, the people; not foreigners, as many people labelled our mainland colleagues. I remember the first time I went to Wesleyville wearing a Mounted Police uniform. I couldn't get a place to stay. While many of the duties we had previously undertaken were now being done by newly appointed civil servants, we were not as stringent in our approach to the many problems people brought to us. For example; if people came in and wanted letters written to government officials, we tried to accommodate them. There are many similar examples of borderline policing.

In those days also, even after 1950, there was lots of overtime; none of it was paid. We worked all day, and all night if necessary, and didn't stop our investigations because we thought our shift was over. The holiday season was always great for the people; but not for the police. Until I retired from the police after twenty years, I never really enjoyed Christmas or New Years. Except for the brief pleasure of gift giving within my family, it was a time of dread. Amidst all the pleasures of the holiday season, there is always trouble. I do not recall having one peaceful Christmas or New Year in twenty years. Nevertheless, not all of the problems were stressful.

Just before Christmas, I think it was 1953, I was apprehensively sitting in my office one evening trying to catch up on some paperwork. There were several functions taking place that evening including a Christmas concert at the one-room Salvation Army School.

About 9:00 o'clock the phone rang. It was the old fashioned phone which required several long and short rings, and allowed everybody to listen in. It was a frantic call from the school. I responded immediately and arrived there within minutes since the school was only a short distance away. Upon arrival, I discovered that Santa Claus was attending the Christmas Concert and had got into a little scuffle with a couple of members of the audience.

The place was in an uproar; in jumping down off the stage, Santa had tipped over the tree. In the melee, the stove had been tipped over; fortunately, there was little fire in it, and it was put out quickly. One elderly lady had fainted, driving her foot through the school window and sustained a cut on her ankle. Because of the confusion, and the crying children, I summarily whisked Santa Claus out of the building, and locked him up.

Returning quickly to the school, calm was restored and whatever could be salvaged of the concert was completed. My investigation concluded that Santa — whom I knew was very shy and reluctant to play the part, but had been convinced to do so by his wife — had, unknown to his religious wife, fortified himself with a few drinks. His buddies, who also attended the concert, continuously made snide and crude remarks. A combination of the booze, heat and uncomplimentary remarks were more than Santa could bear. As a result, he lost his jolly demeanour.

It was the first time, to my knowledge, that Santa Claus had ever been arrested; or even stopped by a traffic cop. I was appalled at what I had done, and felt low and mean for many years thereafter.

But, to my great credit, since it helps assuage my guilt, I realized that Santa Claus could not remain in jail. What would all the children of the world do? It is true that Santa's reputation was sadly tarnished in that community, but all the other children would learn nothing of it unless he was convicted in a court of law. It was too great a burden of guilt for me to carry for the rest of my life; the children would no longer believe in Santa Claus!

I kept Santa in jail for a couple of hours; sufficient for him to soberly reflect on his misdeeds, and then let him go.

He must have behaved impeccably ever since, as I have not heard a word against him in all those years. Rudolph was red-faced with embarrassment then; but Santa Claus has since been fully rehabilitated. Discretion was properly exercised.

POTPOURRI

ZANE GREY'S CABIN

Most western buffs are great admirers of Louis L'Amour, who was a prolific writer. Those who prefer to sit and watch are great fans of John Wayne. In keeping with our current taste for violence both L'Amour and Wayne keep us satisfied. The trend to earthy language and graphic violence is a fairly recent phenomenon. It is only since the 1960s that the majority of the general public have accepted current standards.

Perhaps those few who have read Chaucer, De Maupassant and other earlier authors would disagree. However, it was the Victorian era which placed its strongest stamp on literature and the theatre; we have only recently got over it. Most writing, during that era, used polite speech and the relationships between people were portrayed in a more noble vein. Heroes and heroines appeared to interact with naivete and only the purest motives. Many examples can be recalled with ease.

Zane Grey was a great western novelist, perhaps the greatest, despite his adhering to the Victorian formula. His villains, heroes and heroines were written in classic molds. His scenic descriptions show, not only a vast knowledge of geography, but an outdoors man's appreciation of nature and the world. The references to the gear and equipment, as well as the techniques of use, clearly show that he knew what he was talking about; he had seen and done those things. He hunted, fished and camped all over the world.

Of course Grey could afford it, because not only was he a successful author, he was married to a very wealthy woman, who gave both moral and financial support throughout his life. During his life from, 1872 to 1939, he wrote and published over sixty books; selling over thirteen million copies. Many of his books were on salt and fresh water fishing and were based on his own experiences. I have a collection of his books and have read them several times. It is easy to see that Grey was a superb outdoors man.

You are perfectly right in beginning to wonder what all that has to do with Newfoundland and Labrador. But it has! Zane Grey used to come to Newfoundland to fish for salmon on the Great Codroy River. I suspect that he also fished the Humber as well, though there is probably no one now alive to remember it. I learned about his fishing trips by chance, when I was stationed in the Codroy Valley as a member of the Newfoundland Ranger Force during the winter of 1948-49.

Unlike most places in Newfoundland at that time, there was a network of gravel roads around the Valley. You could get off the Newfoundland Express at Doyle's, or St. Andrews, and travel to Searston, Upper Ferry, O'Regan's, Millville, Codroy and Cape Anguille by car or truck; though there were not many of them. The roads were not ploughed in the winter and travel was by horse and sleigh. The Codroy Valley was a very prosperous farming area, selling its produce, meat and wool all over Newfoundland. The United States Air Force base at Stephenville was a major customer.

Unfortunately, like many things, following our joining Canada, the prosperous farms became fallow. Our farmers were unable to withstand the removal of customs barriers and the onslaught of competition from mainland farmers, who'd had almost a hundred years of subsidies and other forms of support.

As older citizens will remember, travel by horse and sleigh was a slow process; especially when the Ranger had to stop at numerous places to do his work. As a result, we would stop overnight at one of the farms. One of my favourite places was Uncle Mike McIsaac's at Upper Ferry. He was an old man then, in terms of chronological age, but both he and Mrs. McIsaac were active, intelligent and very interesting people.

I always enjoyed staying there as the food was excellent, the atmosphere cosy, and the District Nurse boarded there.

One stormy evening, we were sitting by the blazing stove in their cosy kitchen having a grand chat. I'm sure you know how conversations flow around, and drift from topic to topic. It is difficult to remember now how it came up, but someone must have mentioned reading, and then we talked about western novels and I said now much I enjoyed Zane Grey. Uncle Mike showed obvious interest and said, "You won't believe it, but I knew Zane Grey." I was now all ears and asked him how that came about. He told me that he used to guide foreign sportsmen when he was younger, and had been Zane Grey's guide many times. He said Grey had a cabin at the Overfall Pool on the Great Codroy River. When I said that I understood Grey had been a good outdoors man, Uncle Mike told us that as a guide, he rarely had to do anything except be there. He said Zane Grey could do anything that was required, and enjoyed looking after himself; he was a real sportsman and not at all like many who came there. You can appreciate why that evening has remained in my memory all these years.

Zane Grey used to cross the Gulf from North Sydney, Nova Scotia, and take the train from Port aux Basques to the Overfall Pool. That was not a scheduled stop, but I used to fish there also and the Express train always stopped to accommodate fishermen; we were more civilized and people-conscious in those days.

Now that the Trans-Canada Highway passes by you can identify the Overfall Pool by remembering that when you are travelling towards Port aux Basques you note the following: (a) You pass South Branch along the Great Codroy River until you come to (b) Mollychicnik Brook, and shortly past it, (c) you come to Chicnik Lodge, then (d) you see Overfall Brook. About a hundred yards past Overfall Brook on the right hand side of the highway you'll see a stone fireplace and chimney. That was where Zane Grey's cabin stood. It was just up the

Zane Grey's cabin site
Overfall Pool, Codroy River

riverbank in a fringe of trees; now between the river and the highway; no trouble to see it when the leaves have fallen.

Of course, I wouldn't be able to legally attest to Zane

Grey's title, or even follow the chain of owners since he last came to fish in Newfoundland. I only know what Uncle Mike McIsaac told me; that is sufficient proof for me!

In the spring of 1992 my better half and I went to Arizona for a holiday. That may seem a coincidence; but I knew Zane Grey spent many years of his life there, except for those occasions when he travelled to various parts of the world. He had a cabin in the Tonto Basin, near Payson; which is not all that far from Phoenix. You may be surprised to learn that we made a pilgrimage to the Tonto Basin.

It is beautiful country; not as spectacular as Sedona or the Grand Canyon, but high rugged country of pine forests. Grey's original cabin, as is always the case, had fallen into disrepair. It was restored to its original state a few years before, but unfortunately was destroyed in a forest fire in 1990. That was where Zane Grey wrote most of his books and his burned and twisted typewriter was there in the ruins, amongst other things. I salvaged a few twisted nails and some melted glass; small items which would not arouse suspicion in the minds of Canada Customs.

With all the attention on tourism, it is a great pity that Zane Grey's cabin site on the Great Codroy is not better known. Someone should look into it, before some unthinking environmentalist demolishes the 'Grey' stone fireplace.

THE STEAMSHIP KYLE

I wonder how the S.S. *Kyle* got her name? Many such things are obscured in the mists and fogs of history and can only be the subject of speculation. Others can be solved by patient research or, in its absence, by the application of common sense. Newfoundland has many dialects; though Canadians think we only speak bad English. In the absence of reliable research material, common sense tells me that the *Kyle* got her name because of a misunderstanding in Newcastle upon Tyne when she was christened.

Older Newfoundlanders and Labradorians well remember the expression, "straight off the *coil*." In recent years that has been quoted as, "straight off the *Kyle*." In actual fact, the saying comes from nautical language and really means, not secondhand; fresh; previously uncut; providing a brand new commodity. You see in our vernacular '*kyle*' was what is known as '*coil*' in 'proper' English; uncut from a new coil of rope! There is a story that the *Kyle* was named after a small town in Scotland. Why would the Reids from Newfoundland call one of their ships after a small town in Scotland? I prefer my own version.

We have done the same thing without malice in pronouncing place names; to wit, Jack's Fountain instead of Jacques Fontaine; Bony Experience instead of Bonne Esperance. With names; Gustaf Abel became Goodstuff Abel, Pontius Pilate was pronounced Punchus Pilot, and there are numerous other examples, such was 'upstrapless' for obstreperous. That was what the old fishermen and others said. As long as people understood what they were talking about, everything was fine. It is a small wonder that Giovanni Caboto has become known as John Cabot who discovered this fair land.

The variations in pronunciation, and later spelling, came about innocently enough. It was never the result of Government policy, as is now the case with Canada's official languages. For example, we would never deliberately change a widely known name as a matter of policy. Nova Scotia, Prince Edward Island, British Columbia and Newfoundland have been known throughout the world as such for centuries. Yet they are now officially Novelle-Ecosse, Ile-du-Prince-Edouard, Terra-Neuve and Columbie-Britannique. Alberta, Manitoba, Saskatchewan, Ontario and Quebec remain unchanged; and rightly so. What arrogance! What unmitigated gall to change place names to conform to a perceived linguistic right! It hardly seems to be the result of bilingual policy. But we won't go further into that quicksand now; I merely mention it in order to bring common sense into play.

The *Kyle* was built at Newcastle upon Tyne; a famous shipbuilding centre in the north of England. She was launched in 1913 and sailed to Newfoundland to be delivered to her owners, the Reid Newfoundland Company. The term 'state of the art' was certainly applicable to the *Kyle* for she had the latest coal-fired steam engines, was built for ice-breaking, and had luxurious accommodations for that period. The mahogany and oak panelling gave the ship a rich glow, enhanced by the brass fittings which were polished daily. There was a music room, smoking room, excellent dining facilities and a second class 'steerage' area. She was one of a fleet of ships which sailed the waters around Newfoundland and Labrador. Perhaps the most famous ship was the *Caribou*, mainly because she was tragically torpedoed in the Gulf on October 14th 1942 . The *Kyle* replaced the *Caribou* on the Gulf in winter and provided a vital link to Canada.

It is safe to say, however, that of all the 'coastal boats' the *Kyle* was the most popular, touched more people and places, and will be remembered longer. She sailed for the Reids from

1913 to 1923; for the Newfoundland Government Railway from 1923 to 1949 and for the Canadian National Railways from 1949 to 1959. That year she was decommissioned and sold to Shaw Steamships of Halifax. They renamed her '*Arctic Eagle.*' In 1961 Earle Brothers of Carbonear, bought and used her as a freighter and sealing ship and restored her original name. In 1967 she was at anchor off the Earle premises, lying idle. During a gale on the 2nd of February that year, her anchor chain broke and she drifted into the bottom of the harbour at Riverhead, Harbour Grace, where she lies grounded at low tide. As the old sailors say, "She was left there to die!" Sadly; that is the fate of old people, when they have outlived their usefulness; a higher form of garbage!

Perhaps we can aid in providing a degree of immortality for the *Kyle*. In the traditional religious sense, we know how to attain that blessed state. Perhaps we may be doubtful at times, especially in the case of ships, but there is a more practical way to look at it. It seems to me that there are three basic routes to immortality: (1) Through our children, who will perpetuate our line; (2) Through some outstanding ability such as art, literature, or outstanding deeds; Winston Churchill comes to mind; (3) Our grave marker, headstone, crypt, or tomb. The great pyramid of Cheops is a graphic example. All of these aid successive memory; in human terms, the only way to attain immortality. Writing of, not by, the S.S. *Kyle* may have the same effect; for ships are semi-human.

A few years ago a friend from Newcastle upon Tyne came to visit us in Newfoundland. She was a war-bride and came to Newfoundland via Halifax and North Sydney on the *Kyle*. It was with a degree of shame that we showed her the lonely and abandoned *Kyle* at Harbour Grace.

The Town of Harbour Grace has produced a brochure which claims to give the history of the *Kyle*. Unfortunately it shows that famous ship as being owned by Canadian National Railways from 1923 to 1958. Apparently this is based on the fact that there was a contract between the Government of Canada and the Reid Newfoundland Company for the carriage of mail. The authors inferred from this contract that the *Kyle* belonged to Canadian National Railways. Labrador Airways currently has a contract for the carriage of mail to coastal Labrador; everybody knows this does not transfer ownership of that well-known airline. It seems the unwitting revisionists forget the fact that Newfoundland did not become part of Canada until 1949. I suppose they can hardly be blamed because frequent 'facts' shown on 'Today in History' also ignore the confirmed fact that we were not always part of Canada.

I also harbour many memories of the *Kyle*, especially of trips to and from Labrador. When I left Deer Lake during the War to enlist in the Royal Canadian Air Force, it was the *Kyle* which transported me safely from Port aux Basques to North Sydney. My return journey, following discharge, was also on the *Kyle*. When I first arrived in that foreign country, Canada, they permitted me 'landed immigrant' status; it was the only legal way I could get in. However, it was not until 1949 that I became a Canadian Citizen; thanks to an amendment to the Immigration Act, which accommodated Newfoundlanders and Labradorians.

John Cabot's voyage was not the only voyage of discovery; I discovered the Labrador on the S.S. *Kyle*. Every trip is a voyage of discovery to those who have never been there before. Those who have, or who witness the arrival of the Cabots and Goodyears of this world, should never be offended when we say we have 'discovered' something. It is merely a figure of speech and does not, in any way, discount the prior presence of others. The Goodyears were early explorers, the first one arriving to Newfoundland in 1613. The Micmacs were also explorers; they came to Newfoundland around 1715 from Cape Breton; we arrived here between the Beothucks and Micmacs.

Captain Connors was the master of the *Kyle* when I went

from St. John's to Battle Harbour to take up my duties as a Newfoundland Ranger. It was a real holiday; good food, interesting people and scenic ports of call. The crew were most friendly and obliging; almost like a family taking you into their home. Aside from the three gourmet meals, there was morning coffee, afternoon tea and midnight lunch.

At Trinity, Catalina, Lewisporte and St. Anthony the ship docked at the local wharf. In all other places she anchored off and the mailboat was launched from its davits almost before the anchor was let go. The speed and style of the mailboat crew could easily have drawn praise from the Royal Navy.

When we dropped anchor off the rock which bars the tickle known as Battle Harbour, we were amazed at the number of boats lying-to in wait. Others approached from all directions. The arrival of the *Kyle* was no surprise to local people since, except for Stan Brazil the Marconi operator, most people tracked her approach from the coal smoke trailing behind her. It was a social event which I later saw repeated numerous times. Everybody seemed to know everybody else, the crew being no exception. Boats were tied everywhere around the ship, with the biggest concentration around the gangway; this had been lowered to accommodate passengers and visitors. Freight was soon being hoisted over the side into the waiting boats. It was a skilful, risky business, although no one appeared to be conscious of legal liability.

As I stood on the shore, in what to me was a lonely place, watching the *Kyle* depart, I was consoled by the fact that this familiar friend would be back in about a week. Having met Sgt. Morris Christian and his wife Emma, who took me to my boarding house, I soon felt at home. Molly and Charlie Mangrove were nice people. I am sure Molly could have made a delicious meal out of an old tire, if she had seen one.

Battle Harbour was a busy place in the summer, with much shipping. Fishing schooners could be seen frequently beating their way under sail, or chugging slowly along with underpowered engines when it was calm. My job was to act as a Customs Officer; entering and clearing the salmon boats which plied from Groswater and other Bays, en route to Sydney, Canada, and Boston. Because the whaling industry was in full swing then, I also dealt with the whaling ships which came from Scotland and Norway. These were exciting times for an immature policeman; only each day counted and the future was merely a word in the dictionary.

In those days Battle Harbour was mostly a summer fishing place, though the Marconi operator, the Ranger and a few others lived there year round. The Grenfell Mission had long since moved its hospital to Mary's Harbour; a wintering place for many people. Aside from the ships, two major events stand out in my mind. The first time I ever ate whale steak was aboard the Grenfell hospital boat, the *Maravel*. The other event was a forest fire at Mary's Harbour. Sgt. Christian had gone north on a boat patrol around the district and unfortunately I was in charge. In those days the Ranger was the only Government Official in most rural areas of Newfoundland and Labrador. People came to the Ranger for almost everything from writing a letter to taking charge in a disastrous situation. A boat came from Mary's Harbour to have me take charge of fighting the forest fire. We fought the fire day and night with only fire cans — such as you see in the parks — and shovels. At one time the fire and smoke were so bad that we had to lie in the harbour water. When it was all over, only the hospital and a few houses were left standing. It will never be known if it was the result of an uncontrollable fire, or my incompetence.

There was a vacancy at Nain Detachment and the gods decided I was to transfer there; another friendly trip on the *Kyle*. It was a most enjoyable trip of discovery of Cape Charles, Port Hope Simpson, Hawke Harbour, Pack's Harbour, Batteau, Cartwright and Rigolet; to mention a few on the way north.

As we nosed our way into Hawke Harbour, we could see the whaling factory belching smoke. There was a thick scum on the water; the residue of gutting many whales, and we could see one huge whale on the slip. As the whale was winched up the slip, the men on either side stood with knives shaped like hockey sticks cutting off long strips of blubber. The movement of the whale's carcass assisted in this process. It was not difficult to smell the blubber being rendered into oil; the odour was everywhere. At the invitation of the manager, those of us with strong stomachs went ashore to tour the plant. While there the whistle blew, and all the workers took out their lunch and sat down on the piles of whale meat to eat. We were not as aware of environmental issues then, but I am sure there was ample room for complaint.

Steaming into Rigolet, we saw a small village with gleaming white Hudson's Bay Company buildings, and numerous dogs running down to the spindly wharf. It was a different world from what we had seen on the way up. Mighty Lake Melville emptied into Groswater Bay, with a seven knot tide when it was running in or out.

At Smokey, the antennae of the Marconi Wireless Station could be seen. This was the first place that Admiral Peary and

Sunset on Lake Melville

Captain Bob Bartlett reached, where they could send the message on September 6th 1909 confirming that Peary had reached the North Pole on April 6th. There were many fishing schooners there, as was the case all along the coast. Many of these stops were unscheduled and were made during the fishing season to drop off and pick up mail and freight. It was still in the years when there were hundreds of fishing schooners on the Labrador Coast, from Forteau in the south to Ryan's Bay in the north.

From Smokey to Cape Aillik, Makkovik, Ironbound Islands and in to Hopedale, there were interesting scenes and people. At one stage we were steaming through a huge field of icebergs of every shape and size. Everyone was amazed at their beauty, particularly two Newfoundland passengers who were on their way to Ironbound Islands. One rushed below to fetch his buddy; when the latter came on deck he said "My God, what a size that one is; I wish I had he in a drink."

We finally arrived at Hopedale and anchored, with the same procession of boats and people. This was the transfer point for me, as the *Kyle* turned at Hopedale to work her way back to St. John's. In recent years the coastal boat terminates her trip north at Nain. In the late 1920s the late Richard White was a prosperous trader who lived at Nain, and later Kauk. He used to charter the *Kyle* to pick up him and his family at Nain when they went annually to St. John's on their buying trip. After the stock market crash in 1929, and the 'great depression,' the White's never chartered the *Kyle* again.

I transferred my meagre luggage to the M.V. *Winnifred Lee* for the trip to Nain and went ashore to visit with Ranger Ford. He had been there for two years and was soon due for transfer. This was the first time I had really seen an Eskimo village and its people. Here was a huge two story Moravian Mission building, which housed both the missionaries, and the government store manager's family. It was the second building built to replace the original headquarters which was constructed shortly after 1782, when Hopedale was founded. The second building, still very old, had unique plumbing. This took the form of a two-story indoor toilet, which had only one pit; on the ground floor. When you sat in the ground floor toilet it was possible to hear the person overhead. I imagine many an unknowing person was startled out of deep contemplation.

Everything ashore was new and strange to me; dogs roamed everywhere, but most people paid them scant attention. The houses were hardly up to standards which I was used to, and those standards were not stringent. Everybody was most friendly and greeted me and others in their own language. Ranger Ford told me there was a dance in the village that evening and that we should attend. I was unaware at the time that dances were frowned on by the missionaries; even taboo.

Hence we went to the dance. It was in a small building which I am no longer able to identify, even if it still stands. The place was rocking when we went in and it was something to behold. An old fashioned square dance was in progress with sealskin boots pounding the buckling floorboards; everybody was having a good time. The fiddler, who I learned was Josua Abel, performed non-stop with a woman on either side mopping his brow. A number of members of the *Kyle*'s crew were present. There was no sign of drinking, but I suspect that many of the participants went outside for more than fresh air. Air was certainly necessary, as there were overpowering odours; familiar and new.

The next time I saw the *Kyle* was in August the following year. One of our duties was to escort mental patients to the asylum in St. John's. That unfortunate person was a female from Nain. In order to meet the *Kyle* we travelled in a hired open boat to Hopedale. I was unable to get a matron to travel all the way to St. John's from Nain, and finally persuaded a woman from Hopedale to make the trip. For the record I shall call her Aunt Louisa; she was a reluctant escort.

Our regulations required that all prisoners and mental patients travel second class; that meant 'steerage.' On the way to Labrador the first class accommodation was good, as was the company, and I had no interest in seeing what went on in steerage. By implication, I had to travel down there also. The patient must never be allowed out of the sight of the Matron, or the Ranger. There was always the danger of losing the patient overboard. If that happened, I might as well join her.

The steerage was fairly open space, with long dining tables and many double-decker bunks; something like a floating barracks. It did not seem to segregate men from women, as one would expect in those days. It was not unusual to hear Tarzan's love call in those primitive surroundings.

After my first dining experience I arranged with the matron to relieve me at mealtimes so that I could go on top. It was not that the food wasn't good; it was cooked in the same galley. But the service was hardly the same. The steerage steward was obviously of lower rank than his colleagues. He had an artificial eye and, when washing dishes back there, he often missed the water. At one time he dropped his eye in the dishpan, fished it out, and replaced it. When we arrived at St. John's it was difficult to determine who should be placed in the asylum. Fortunately, during the rest of my service in Labrador, I never had to travel second class again.

On the return voyage I was much rested, having had a brief visit home. It was September when we left St. John's and I had a companion, Ranger Wiseman, who was being trans-ferred to Hopedale. We had a most enjoyable trip as the *Kyle* was packed with people all the way up the coast. The piano and the music played non-stop, and the card games in the smoking room followed suit; we would alternate between one and the other. Amongst the passengers were John R. Grieve and his wife who were on their way to Makkovik, and then to Kaipokok Bay to start a logging operation; they hosted several parties.

Captain Ned O'Keefe had now replaced Captain Connors on the *Kyle*. They were both extremely competent, with different personalities; Ned O'Keefe was very outgoing and friendly. One evening, someone bet the Captain that he couldn't name every port of call for the coastal boats around Newfoundland and Labrador; the prize was a bottle of rum. We took a map, and between sips, Captain O'Keefe named every port of call in sequence, without missing one. It was a tribute to the remarkable sailors who plied the waters off Newfoundland and Labrador; through fog, sleet, snow and ice. They knew every rock and shoal; not only those shown on the nautical charts, but those in places that are 'barred-off' by the chart makers.

That was not my last trip on the *Kyle*, nor the most memorable; there is no need to elaborate further, for I am sure you have tasted the flavour of that good ship. Before the construction of government wharves, airstrips, and the more structured services provided by Canadian National Railways and the Government of Canada, the *Kyle* played a personal role in the lives of people. It was an important social, commercial and political link between the people of Newfoundland and Labrador; whether they realized it or not.

In subsequent years; with the growth of population, more sophistication in transportation and communications, and the rise of native and other political movements, the lesson of the *Kyle* has largely been forgotten. If we are to continue to maintain that anchor chain between Newfoundland and Labrador, and reinforce the links with welding, there must be some re-thinking.

SOME DOGS LIKE TUXEDOS

There are dogs everywhere. Almost every kind, colour and description can be seen around town and country. Dogs are loved, petted, pampered, doctored, hated, feared and abused. We all know of examples. They have increased in number and variety and evidence of their presence can be seen everywhere. Mans' best friend has changed his role, and now persons are dogs' best friend. To judge by the dog food in the supermarkets, more attention is paid to canine than human diet. I suppose, with few exceptions, only their 'owners' know if they are useful or not.

Other countries have experienced the same thing, perhaps to a greater extent. A while ago we were in England, trying to find our roots. Unfortunately, there was great reluctance there to admit we were related. We saw many sights; familiar because of all that British history which was beat into our skulls before Confederation. In many respects it was like going home. But the dogs, they were everywhere. In the cities, in the towns, in the country; you couldn't escape them. They were very productive too. Their products were everywhere; all shapes, sizes and textures.

Now, my favourite dog is the retriever, of whatever make. It keeps you company while hunting alone, enjoys a good conversation without interrupting, frightens timid hunters who don't like dogs and, best of all, brings the ducks back without getting your feet wet. Some dogs I don't like, but won't identify them because I'm sensitive to the feelings of others. Ask your postman his opinion; he might be less restrained.

I met one dog of the class I don't like one summer while fishing down St. Mary's Bay way. Having portaged, paddled and struggled to the upper part of Big Barachois, I set up my camp on the pool. No one in the world but me, so I thought.

I fished for a while, naturally without success. Good fishermen, so they say, never admit to catching anything. It was a nice day for fishing; the peace comfortably broken by the roar of the river. It was overcast, with a drift of drizzle now and then so that the two beavers across the way thought it was later in the day and came out of their lodge. It was the kind of day that the suitably clad outdoors person enjoys, perhaps because it discourages others.

Anyway, the time came to give the pool a rest. After priming the Optimus, I was soon sitting on a rock watching the pool between sips and swallows. There was not a move, except for three gulls and the beavers some distance away.

When you have lots of time it's important for your health and well-being to make a ritual of everything. Make it last as long as you can because you'll be back in the rat race soon enough. There was no hurry to start fishing again so I pulled out my floating toothbrush and slowly waded out to where my back would have to bend least. What a foolish design for a toothbrush; it would be better for it to sink, because then there would be some hope of retrieval.

I was brushing away, eyeing the pool, and thinking about all that running water, and my well almost dry, when all of a sudden there was a vicious snarling behind me. Fortunately, I was out in the river, armed with my floating toothbrush, because the dog straining on the bank had every appearance of intending to eat me. Imagine how it would feel being attacked when I thought I was all alone in the world.

The dog's companion had come up on his ATV. Its sound was obscured by the wind, woods and river. I didn't make friends with the dog or its 'master.'

One spring we pulled off a big dog rescue, in the cliffs of Torbay. This poor creature was spotted on a ledge, surrounded on three sides by the swirling sea, with a cliff in the back. Apparently he had washed off another ledge and made it to this one, but wouldn't take a chance on another swim. We heard later the dog had been missing for a week.

Well, Sir or Madam, we got out the ropes, climbing boots, hard hats and tried several times to get him up. Finally, with his cooperation, we hauled him up hand over hand in a big canvas hockey bag. Both dog and owner were grateful; a great day. Afterwards, it didn't even take refreshments to keep the conversation going.

During the festive season the other year, I had to go to a formal dinner. It was one of those stag affairs, medals and all. My old tuxedo came out of the closet and was hung out on the clothesline, gasping for air.

When I came home for lunch my wife said, "Did you bring in your pants?" "No, why?" I asked. "Well, they're gone." Sure enough, they were. Now what good is a tuxedo without pants? More especially since every man, and his dog, has a different style, colour and fabric. Well, I had to rent a pair, even though they didn't match. The difference between the pants and jacket was easy to explain, though hard to believe.

You guessed it, my wife found those pants in the possession, and on the property of, the dog we rescued, and his 'owner.' They had been chewed beyond wearability.

Was it the retriever's instinct? Is it all foolishness that a dog never forgets a kindness? Perhaps that dog thought he was doing me a favour because those pants were out of style. The dog never would tell me, and the owner remained silent also. In the end I had to replace them at my own expense; so much for gratitude.

I am sure dogs are great for those who own them, or would like to own them. But, uncontrolled they are like everything else. I believe there are dog control laws which require only an honest effort at enforcement. Perhaps it is time those in authority put their foot down. But, on second thought.....